The BluePrint of a ThriveHER

From Surviving To Thriving

Copyright @ 2024 Dr. Sonya Alise McKinzie

Cover Design by Ra'Nesha Taylor

No part of this journal may be reproduced, distributed, or transmitted in any form or by any means including photocopying or by any electronic methods without written permission from the publisher. For permission requests, write to the publisher addressed, "Attention: Permission Department," at the address below or via email.

P.O. Box EE-16967
Winners Avenue Books
New Providence
The Bahamas
winwithwinneravenuebooks@gmail.com

ISBN: 9798325799945

Printed in the United States of America

Table Of Contents

Dedication..05

Foreword
Dr. Wanda R. W. McKinley....................................... 06

Introduction
Dr. Sonya Alise McKinzie 13

Joni Ellis Bodie
Stepping Through Life with Mercy and Grace 20

Tara Lindsay-Ferguson
When I No Longer Saw Myself In The Mirror................ 32

Barbara Green
Healing in His Word: A Woman's Triumph Over Abuse 41

Alexandria Johnson
I Took Back My Power!..52

Dr. Cheryl Kehl
Bounced Back and Healed... 62

Joanne B. Lewis
I.am.Enough..73

Dr. Sonya Alise McKinzie
Shattering Shackles: Whispers In The Twilight 83

Lisa Pearce
From Bondage To Deliverance 100

April Randall
My Friend, Anna... 111

Maresa Roach
Thriving From The Heart Of Hurt 128

Ra'Nesha Taylor
A Journey of Healing and Self-Reclamation.........................141

Dedication

"This book is dedicated to all the supporters of the Blueprint of a ThriveHER Book Collaboration. Your unwavering faith, relentless support, and invaluable contributions have been the cornerstone of this endeavor.

As we journey together in this collaboration, let us remember the words from the Bible, Proverbs 27:17, "As iron sharpens iron, so one person sharpens another." Your insights and experiences have indeed sharpened our perspectives and enriched this book.

We also find strength in Ecclesiastes 4:9-10, "Two are better than one, because they have a good return for their labor: If either of them falls down, one can help the other up." This collaboration is a testament to the power of unity and shared vision.

May this book serve as a source of hope and a blueprint for thriving, just as Jeremiah 29:11 promises, "For I know the plans I have for you," declares the LORD, "plans to prosper you and not to harm you, plans to give you hope and a future."

Thank you for being a part of this journey. Your support has made all the difference."

Foreword
Dr. Wanda R. W. McKinley

Dr. Wanda McKinley has been a part of the Dallas community for over 30 years. Her family relocated here from California when her father retired from the Navy. She has been educating families for over 30 years in the Healthcare, Insurance, and Mental Health Industry, believing that knowledge is power. In November 2013, God showed Dr. McKinley her purpose in life. Being a survivor of domestic violence, God told her that she must be transparent with men, women, and children by sharing her story so that they would find comfort in her. Dr. McKinley was a victim of abuse for over 24 consecutive years. Her biological father molested her from the age of seven.

Eventually, it escalated to sexual penetration at the age of thirteen after her stepfather raped her taking her virginity, and the rape continued to the age of eighteen by both men. Dr. McKinley met her ex-husband at nineteen and married at twenty-four. She suffered physical, mental, verbal, sexual, and financial abuse for eleven years. Dr. McKinley also was raped by a classmate and molested by an uncle. Many different men use her for their self-pleasure.

Through the grace of God, she survived. Her calling and passion are to help others. We are Survivors was formed as an international 501©3 non-profit organization for abused men, women, and children. Its mission is to provide a stable environment for abused and battered individuals by providing temporary shelter, professional counseling, and employment training. We want to help them transition from abusive situations to being self-sufficient people in society. Understanding the pain on a personal level helps her relate to the men, women, and children God sends to her.

Dr. McKinley is a best-selling author, domestic and international, a recipient of an International Humanitarian Award, 2016 Advocate of the Year for Domestic Violence, and a strong Domestic and International speaker who has traveled to Germany, London, Finland, and Africa. She received an Honorary International Doctorate Degree in Social Advocacy in 2020 due to her work in the United States and Internationally. Dr. McKinley has an international television show called We are Survivors that can be viewed on FMD Global TV on ROKU TV. Dr. McKinley has also launched an apparel line called ROAR and We are Survivors Book Series through her LLC named Hear Me ROAR which focuses on domestic violence. Dr. McKinley has also been named 2017-2018 and 2018-2019 Who's Who in Black Dallas and Who's Who in America for 2024. Dr. McKinley is also the CEO of McKinley Counseling Firm.

Once a licensed clinical mental health therapist, McKinley Counseling Firm was born, and Dr. McKinley began to work with individuals and families, helping them with life's challenges through therapy and hypnosis. Its focus is on empowering, mentoring, and educating. In the year 2022, Dr. McKinley purchased a franchise called Maze of Life, which works with individuals who have been court-ordered to attend anger management and domestic violence classes as part of the rehabilitation process. Believing in God and hearing Him only has carried her thus far. Dr. McKinley is a child of God and has embraced what He has for her. May God be given all the glory as she continues helping and educating His people.

With great honor and profound respect, I introduce "The Blueprint of a ThriveHer," a remarkable work by Dr. Sonya Alise McKinzie. This book chronicles the lives of twelve extraordinary women and is a testament to resilience, faith, and the transformative power of shared experiences. As you embark on this journey through their stories, you will find yourself inspired, moved, and, most importantly, uplifted by the collective strength and grace these women embody.

Dr. Sonya Alise McKinzie is a beacon of hope and a paragon of leadership. Her vision for this book was not just to tell the stories of these women but to create a blueprint for thriving despite adversity. Dr. McKinzie's journey is woven with perseverance, faith, and an unwavering commitment to uplifting others. Her dedication to this project stems from a deeply rooted belief that every challenge these women face is an opportunity to demonstrate the incredible power of the human spirit when guided by divine purpose.

Born and raised in a modest community, Dr. McKinzie's early life was shaped by a strong sense of family and faith. Her parents instilled in her the values of hard work, integrity, and compassion. These foundational principles guided her through her educational and professional pursuits, culminating in a distinguished career as a scholar, mentor, and advocate. Dr. McKinzie's academic achievements are numerous, but her heart for service and her ability to inspire others truly set her apart.

"The Blueprint of a ThriveHer" is not just a book but a movement. Dr. McKinzie was inspired to unite twelve women whose lives reflect a spectrum of adversities and triumphs. Each story is a powerful narrative of overcoming, resilience, and faith. These women have faced challenges ranging from personal loss and health crises to professional setbacks and societal barriers. Yet, they have emerged more vigorous, determined, and compassionate in every instance. Their stories are a testament to the indomitable human spirit and the profound impact of faith.

Dr. McKinzie's approach to this project was both innovative and deeply personal. She spent countless hours listening to, documenting, and understanding each woman's unique experiences. Her ability to capture their voices with authenticity and sensitivity reflects her deep empathy and commitment to honoring their journeys. Dr. McKinzie believes that by sharing these stories, she can help others find hope, strength, and a sense of community.

Central to this book is the idea that thriving is not just about overcoming adversity but finding purpose and joy in the journey. Dr. McKinzie emphasizes that each woman's story is a blueprint for others to follow. These blueprints are not prescriptive but rather illustrative, showing that while our paths may differ, resilience, faith, and community principles are universal. Readers will find practical wisdom, spiritual insights, and a renewed sense of hope through these narratives.

One of the most compelling aspects of "The Blueprint of a ThriveHer" is the diversity of the women's experiences. Dr. McKinzie has curated a collection of stories that reflect various backgrounds, professions, and life stages. This diversity is intentional and highlights the universal applicability of the book's core message. Whether you are a young professional facing career challenges, a mother navigating the complexities of family life, or someone seeking to find meaning in the face of loss, you will find a story that resonates with your experiences.

Dr. McKinzie's leadership extends beyond the pages of this book. She is an active mentor and advocate dedicated to empowering women and fostering communities of support. Her work with various organizations and initiatives has had a lasting impact on countless lives. She is a sought-after speaker and a respected voice in women's empowerment, faith, and resilience discussions. Her ability to connect with others deeply and personally has made her a beloved figure in her community and beyond.

In "The Blueprint of a ThriveHer," Dr. McKinzie also explores the role of faith in overcoming adversity. For many of the women featured in this book, their faith was a source of strength and guidance. Dr. McKinzie herself attributes much of her resilience to her faith. She believes a solid spiritual foundation is crucial for navigating life's challenges. This book is, therefore, not just a celebration of human strength but also a testament to the power of divine guidance.

As you read through the stories of these twelve incredible women, you will be struck by their honesty, courage, and vulnerability. Dr. McKinzie has created a space where their voices can be heard, their experiences validated, and their wisdom shared. This book is an invitation to join a community of ThriveHers—women who support, inspire, and uplift one another.

In closing, "The Blueprint of a ThriveHer" is more than a collection of stories; it is a call to action. Dr. McKinzie urges us to look beyond our struggles and to see the potential for growth and transformation in every challenge. She reminds us that we are not alone and that sharing our stories can create a ripple effect of hope and empowerment.

Dr. Sonya Alise McKinzie's vision, passion, and unwavering faith have brought this project to life. Her dedication to highlighting the strength and resilience of women is evident on every page. As you delve into this book, may you be inspired by the stories of these remarkable women, and may you find your blueprint for thriving. Dr. McKinzie's message is clear: no matter what you face, you have the power to overcome and thrive. This book is your guide, companion, and source of inspiration. Welcome to the world of ThriveHers.

With most profound respect and admiration,

Dr. Wanda R.W. McKinley

Dr. Sonya Alise McKinzie
Visionary Author

Sonya McKinzie is a humanitarian at heart who has always felt a strong passion for helping and serving people from different backgrounds. She is a 20-plus-year-old ThriveHER of domestic violence, a Certified Trauma and Recovery Life Coach, a Certified Domestic Violence Advocate, and a Senior Client Success Manager. She lives in Cumming, GA, with her wonderful 13-year-old old daughter (McKinzie Alise Baker), whom she considers her greatest gift from God. Sonya's personal and family history of abuse led her to reclaim her life and voice after surviving domestic violence. In her early twenties, she faced suicidal thoughts , but she turned her pain into resilience and became a source of hope and encouragement for others in need. In 2003, she left her hometown, Brunswick, GA, to escape from her abuser. That is when she began to transform from a victim to a victor.

Sonya pursued self-improvement and inner peace in her journey. Driven by her faith and ambition, she sought new career opportunities but realized that her education was a limiting factor. She did not let that stop her, and she continued her studies, earning degrees in Business Administration (A.A.), Business Management (B.A.), and Human Services Counseling (M.A.), with minors in addictions & recovery. She also obtained five certifications in various fields related to human services: Victims Advocacy, Corporate Leadership and Management, Call Center Management, Six Sigma (Green Belt), and Human Resources. Dr. Sonya received an honorary Doctorate in Humanitarianism from GIA.

She is also an alumna of cohort #171, Nasdaq Entrepreneurial Center. Besides her academic accomplishments, Sonya also has a Master's in Communication, is a Certified Life Coach and is one of the faces of Marsy's Law for All. She has written 13 books, mostly about healing and coping with the challenges of surviving and thriving after trauma and abuse. She has a wealth of knowledge and experience in her advocacy work. She has also supported her daughter's passions and desires to be an author and is known as the Lil' ThriveHER, which is chronicled in 3 of her 5 books. Like her mother, McKinzie believes in respect and diversity and strives to be a beacon of light to children who are change agents for little girls under the

Girls of Virtue Program under the ThriveHER Inc. umbrella.

She is the Founder and Executive Director of ThriveHER Incorporated (formerly known as Women of Virtue Transitional Foundation), which she established in February 2016. She followed her divine vision to create a platform that exposes the signs of domestic violence and abuse in a raw, real, and transparent way. Through her words, she has bridged the gap between the public/community, survivors, victims, and their families, and has given voice to the courage of domestic victors (often mislabeled as victims). The organization hosts several events throughout the year to raise awareness and funds for empowerment programs and services, build professional partnerships, and donate to affiliated organizations. As the trademark holder of ThriveHER, Sonya has been fighting for her rights to the trademark due to infringement and is advocating for the recognition of her original work that honors women of abuse and redefines the image of "survivors" who are thriving in their survivorship. She wrote Thrive-HER in 2017 and secured the trademark in 2019. She is known for her warm, intimate brunches and fundraisers, where she uses the trademark as a defining symbol of change in her community. In 2020, Sonya had a vision of creating a movement that would change the way people perceive survivors of trauma; however, she did not see her vision come to life until December 2023, when she decided to push forward with her mission.

Introduction

Hey y'all, how are you doing today?

Are you having a hard day, perhaps struggling to make it from one point to another? Trust me, I understand. To be honest, I more than understand.

We all go through the valleys now and again, and for this reason, I know there is something in this book for you. Just a little something to guide you towards your breakthrough.

Can I take a few minutes of your time before we reach the core parts of this book? I want to share some beautiful and not-so-beautiful things with yall.

Welcome to "The Blueprint of a ThriveHER," a book that is more than just pages bound together—it's a journey, a testament, and a beacon of hope for those who have faced life's storms and are seeking a path to triumph.

In these pages, we are extending a warm, Southern greeting and an invitation to pause, reflect, and connect. With a narrative as comforting as a conversation on a front porch swing, I beckon you into a world where hardships are acknowledged, tears are shared, and laughter echoes through the chapters of resilience.

Raised in the steadfast faith of a Baptist church and guided by the unwavering spirit of a praying grandmother, I didn't always grasp the power of scripture. Yet, as I stand today—as a visionary and coauthor—weaving scriptures into the fabric of this collaborative masterpiece.

This book is a tapestry of experiences, interlaced with the strength and vulnerability of twelve extraordinary women who have together shed tears, found joy, and offered prayers. Our bond transcends the pages of this collaboration, for we are divinely connected, and our project ordained by God.

Candidly, we are sharing the genesis of this endeavor, a vision birthed in 2020 but hesitantly embraced. It was a call to lead, to unite, and to inspire—a call that I initially fled from, burdened by self-doubt and the daunting task of rallying others to a shared cause. Yet, in stillness, I found my calling and the courage to serve.

"The Blueprint of a ThriveHER" is not merely a book; it's a mission to uplift women who have weathered trauma, adversity, and trials. It's about extending a hand, offering a shoulder, and whispering prayers of strength and solace. It's about transforming from victims into victors, from survivors into ThriveHERs.

The co-authors of "The Blueprint of a ThriveHER" are a group of inspiring women who have joined me in this empowering project. Each co-author brings her own unique "BEEN-THROUGH" story to support others in reaching their "BREAK THROUGH." They have been carefully selected to create a safe and empowering space, sharing their transformational and powerful testimonies to help break chains and plant seeds of faith for those on their healing journeys from surviving to thriving.

The co-authors have been part of this journey, not just as writers, but as partners in healing, sharing their experiences, and supporting one another through the process. Their collective efforts have resulted in a book that is not only a collection of stories but a movement toward empowerment and growth.

So, as you turn these pages, know that you are not alone. You are part of a larger story, a collective heartbeat, a chorus of voices rising in unison to declare that from the ashes of struggle, we can all emerge stronger, wiser, and thriving. Welcome to the blueprint of your breakthrough.

Joni Ellis Bodie

Joni Ellis Bodie lives in Southeast Georgia and is a Child of God and an avid nature lover that loves to walk the trails at state parks and historical sites. She has a BA in English Literature and is a member of the Alpha Chi National College Honor Society. She is presently working to complete her Master's in Clinical Counseling. She is an advocate for women's rights and the homeless, people and animals. The first half of her life she jumped from one abusive type of relationship to another, from childhood into three marriages until finally she had enough, and God sat her down. It was through her love of words that she got past trauma and grief and is now stepping out to share her story. She believes that "One is never too old to learn something new or start a new thing" and lives every day believing that with God and through prayer anything is possible.

Be strong and courageous. Do not fear or be in dread of them, for it is the LORD your God who goes with you. He will not leave you or forsake you.— Deuteronomy 31:6.

Connect with her a jawga_belle@ yahoo.com.

Stepping Through Life With Mercy and Grace

Joni Ellis Bodie

My story has its roots in what most would consider an idyllic childhood in the 60s in an upper-middle-class home with a family that went to church, enjoyed family vacations, and had Sunday dinners where we all gathered. My daddy was a big man in town but as I grew toward my teen years, there was a darkness growing in our home that few knew about. My parents, who drank socially began to drink more heavily, and fighting and screaming became the nightly noise in our home. Domestic violence comes in many forms of abuse; it can be physical, emotional, mental, financial, sexual, and come as coercive control.

My story has touches of a few of these, but I grew up unaware that what we/I were/was going through was anything as dark and scarring as it was and would be carried into my adult life. My mother was an alcoholic, she drank to self-medicate as I found out later in life. Mental issues were not considered to be normal and treatable conditions in those days. For women, it was most often diagnosed as "hormonal issues", and they were given hormones, and told to get control of their emotions but the real problems went untreated. My father was a drinker as well, but high functioning. He too had psychological issues but refused to see them, he considered mental illness a weakness, one that had no place in his life.

I grew up trying to protect my sisters from the nightly hollering and fighting, as well as the spankings for bad behavior. The idyllic life became punctuated with times when, because of differences due to drinking and fighting, my father would forbid us to see our grandparents. We would be wary to invite friends over as well. This abuse was emotional and psychological; as a teen, I began to feel isolated and alone. When the drinking increased and the chaos at home grew, so did the domestic abuse issues. The amazing revelation as I see it now was that no one outside of our family saw what was happening, no one knew we were living anything but this idyllic life. I will say our grandparents and the need to put forth a normal and happy front socially was a blessing. That and our Church and involvement in choir, Sunday school, and MYF were what built my faith into the foundation it was and still is in my life.

The control issues and degradation that came with the ongoing cycle of abuse from my parents put me in a place where I decided that the only way I could get away from the chaos and live a peaceful life was to study and escape by going to college. I would never have to look back then; an education would be my saving grace. I survived the abuse at home, I thrived in it by putting my energy into schoolwork and making the grades to escape to college. But I was soon to find out that even that would not be easy.

So many of us wonder how some people end up where they are, how things change for them, how one event makes life go off the rails and they end up in an unexpected place. For me I know, I know the minute that life changed from my dream to the life that would be mine for the next 20 years. It was the morning I left home in my packed car to go to Middle Georgia College to study Journalism. I was excited, so excited, I saw nothing but adventure and a new beginning before me. I believed I had broken free from the control and craziness I had lived in. But that was not to be.

I was in my car, on my CB radio, talking to my boyfriend as I made my way to his house for my goodbye. What happened next was surely nothing I had imagined. As we chatted on the radio, my daddy broke in, he was driving behind me, had heard me, and thought for some reason that I was going to pick up my boyfriend and take him with me to college. This was not "his plan," his control issues and anger were about to define the next 20 years of my life. He had me pull over in the Easy Shop parking lot, he got out of his car and demanded that I do. The next thing I knew he had slapped me so hard I was knocked up against my car. He ordered me to get in my car, he forbade me to go to his house for any reason, he informed me he was following me to Hwy 75 and I was going straight there. Of course, I was in shock, reeling from the slap, and crying because I had no intention of doing what he thought I was. I was on my way to a new life. The past abuse, the control, the mental and emotional abuse that I had endured for so many years all seemed to catch up to me as I drove toward the highway.

As I started down the on-ramp, my daddy's voice, loud and forceful, came through my CB radio, "You are to go to college, you will not defy me ever again" he hollered. I drove crying down the ramp and headed south, my hands shaking, my mind reeling with "how this could be happening" thoughts. Would I never escape this chaos, this abuse, can I not even educate my way to freedom? I then got angry, and scared, and realized I would never be free of him and his control. I took the next exit off the expressway, still distraught and crying I was almost hit by an eighteen-wheeler, so I pulled over on the side of the road, in shock. For the next few minutes, I sat crying, unsure of what to do. My mind racing over the past and in my rage and pain, I decided to drive back to Griffin, to go see my boyfriend. This was when my life took a detour that took me years to correct.

My boyfriend would become my first husband and the father to my two sons. Our relationship was one of innocence and youth in a time when things were not as frightening or as complicated as they are in today's world. It was never really "love" and toxic in the end, there were signs in the beginning, but I did not see them. He would change, and I would too, we were kids when we started this. After the kids were born, we moved to Texas, and my husband's dad got him a trucking job. The opportunity was calling, and we saw it as an adventure.

I was a long way from home when my marriage fell apart. My husband had a new job, and new friends, all of which were single, and I began to drink more and do things I had no idea about. Then one night, it all came to a head, he was fine one minute, and the next, he was beating me up like a prize fighter and I had no idea why. I know that when he hit me something inside of me snapped. Maybe it was the chaos of abuse when I grew up, but I fought back, I fought back to save my life! I just know that if the neighbor had not called the police, I might have died that night. But I would not have gone down without a fight! I waited two weeks to leave him, to recover from the horrible beating. I came home 1300 miles with my kids and what I could pack in my car to start over.

I came home from Texas and after a couple of months of groveling to my daddy and him once again trying to take over my life I was reunited with my first love. He was just another man my daddy would not approve of, but I was not alone. We had a couple of good years until alcohol and his diabetes would change our lives.

We were happy, he loved my kids, and they loved him. He doted on them, took them fishing, and played with them, he was their daddy. We seemed to be doing well when he had an accident at work, he was a roofer, and the tar kettle blew up. His trip to the hospital for his injuries would reveal he needed insulin shots and was a diabetic.

After the accident, he would begin to drink, again, alcohol was a catalyst to abuse in my life. His drinking would cause diabetic blackouts that would end in him beating me up. I would call the cops; they would lock him up and the next day his brother would get him and bring him home. He would wake up in jail and not even remember how he got there but I will stress, this is no excuse. No excuse can ever make abusing anyone in any way right or acceptable. The young me thought love could conquer all of this, he would see the error of his ways. He did not. I did the "put him in jail trick" a few times before I finally decided that this was not going to work, love does not make everything better. After a hard struggle with my heart, I knew I had to divorce him too. Again, my past abuse would cause me to react in a way that would lead me on my way again. But this time there would be an ending I did not see coming.

After there seemed no end to the drinking and abuse, I left and moved in with my best friend and her husband. They had a huge house and offered my boys and me a place to land. One night as we were eating, there was a knock at the door, it was him, drunk. I went out to talk to him because he would not go without talking to me. When I made my way out the door, he was quick to come close and immediately I could smell it. He was pleading with me to come home, and told me that he loved me, and could not live without me. I was telling him it was over; I couldn't do it anymore. The next thing I knew he had a gun in his hand and was telling me if he could not have me, no one else could. He was going to kill us both! We began to struggle and to be honest, had he been any soberer, I am sure I would not be here today writing this. Somehow, he staggered and lost his balance, I grabbed the gun, that was loaded and cocked, and as he fell back, I shot the gun off in the air and bolted in the back door. My friend came running just as my husband came in the door. My friend hit him once and he went down and out. The sheriff came and took him away. Another ending, a sad and frightening one.

This would take me on to the third and final relationship which would be fraught with abuse. This one would not be just physical but mental and emotional as well. You know when you watch the ID channel and they say, "But there had been signs…" Well, there were. At this point, I was not well versed in mental issues and what they meant, but I would learn. This time, it was not alcohol but drugs that would lead to abuse. There was also a much more frightening aspect of stalking and unhinged rage. I was beaten this time to the ground, I crawled to the house shouting for help and my brother-in-law who lived next door came to my rescue. This would not be the end of this husband's reign of terror in my life, but it would be the last time he touched me. He would break into my house when I was gone, follow me, and even scare me at times accusing me of things that were not real. But he was done, I was done, it was over.

The end of my third marriage brought me to the realization that I could not, would not, ever be in the position of abuse again nor would I put my sons through anymore. I would spend the next thirteen years alone, raising my kids and healing my scars leaning on God to carry me and lift me after I had a disabling accident at work. I will always tell anyone who wonders the "how" about my life's trek, it is without a doubt that God has carried me through. It was after my accident that my relationship with my mom and dad would start to truly heal. After both my sons had married and left home, they started telling me I needed to date, and find someone. I ruminated on that for a while and found a surprising relationship with a man I will say was my true love and soulmate.

My fourth marriage was to my Michael. He was a gentle, kind man, who loved me just as I am all scarred and imperfect. We always said we were each other's other half, what one lacked the other had. We spent every day together, and I treasure my memories of him. He passed away too soon but left me with so many gifts. After he died, I got to realize my educational dreams and went to college finally. There is not a day that goes by I do not think of him, he taught me so much. I still talk to him at times, I believe he watches over me, and he is waiting for me to join him one day. So, I am telling you bad relationships do not have to be your forever, there is hope, and God can surprise you!

I have told you all of this so you can see, that an idyllic childhood can be not as idyllic as it seems. The things we do to each other, to our children, the things they hear and see, they all matter. No form of domestic violence and abuse leaves anyone in its shadow unscathed. I want you to take away from this story that I am blessed, I have fallen back on the one constant good thing in my life, GOD, and my foundation of faith. I loved and respected my parents until they died, still do. We grew, we acknowledged some things and left some to lie buried forever. As for my husband, I hold no bad feelings. The first is still alive, he abandoned his kids, and I never looked back. The second one died much too young due to his medical issues, I hated that. The third one, we came back together later in life, and I had a chance to help him, and he helped me. My story has a happy ending because of God. Because He never left me alone, He carried me when I could not walk, and He gave me mercy and grace to become, to be, to go on.

I am evidence of strength and persistence.

Tara Lindsay-Ferguson

Tara Lindsay-Ferguson is native of South Carolina and is a mother to her three amazing children Quasaun, Ti'yanna, and Zacarii. She is the owner of "Hope Services". She obtained her Master's in Health Care Management from Strayer University and a Maaster's in Business Management specializing in Accounting from Nova SE University.

She served as an educator within the Broward County School System. She owned her own daycare and worked in management within various other companies. Currently, she serves as the Dean of the Kingdom United Institute of Learning an online Bible School.

Tara believes in serving her church and community. She is a board member of Full Life Hope Center, a nonprofit organization for displaced individuals and families. She is a member of S.A.L.T (Sister-Anointed-Love & Teach). She serves as an International Missionary with Jesus is King Ministry. She attends Trees of Righteousness Ministry under the leadership of Elder Betty Robinson. She serves with York County and assist various organizations in community events.

She enjoy spending time with her family. She loves traveling and making memories with her mom and children. She believes that without knowledge you can never obtain your full destiny. Connect with her at hope23services@gmail.com.

When I No Longer Saw Myself In The Mirror

Tara Lindsay-Ferguson

In the midst of the storm, there is often a deceptive tranquility that leads the way to the turbulence ahead. Such was the beginning of a relationship that promised harmony but delivered discord. It started seamlessly, a smooth entry into what would become a journey of self-discovery through the trials of being with someone whose path diverged sharply from my own.

As I was sitting here writing this chapter, I began to reflect on the various events that transpired over what seemed to be decades. I am recalling the countless conversations about who I should and should not allow in my space. I remember like it was yesterday when he said, "It's imperative that you distance yourself from certain individuals who are not striving for self-improvement or aligned with your aspirations." He continued to remind me that I needed to use a spirit of discernment because, from his bird's eye view, any person that I engaged with were using me.

Many times, he would warn " There were certain things that he would not tolerate, weight gain is one, and all those church trips are another," he reminded me. He was a perfectionist and pushed me to strive to do and be better.

Whenever I expressed my dreams and desires to him, they were consistently silenced or postponed. So, I sat in limbo, waiting for his arbitrary conditions to be met. Everything had to be under his control and his timing. He lacked compassion, forgiveness, and held a heavy load of judgment over my head.

Our family trips were always my responsibility, and the burdens of planning and financing fell squarely on my shoulders. These excursions were inevitably brief due to his aversion to travel. It was predictable that, upon our arrival, he would have an immediate need for a nap, which dictated our schedule, leaving me to explore solo. While we found joy in familiar routines at home, our trips were marred by his complaints, which I begrudgingly accepted as part of who he was.

At first, I felt I could change some small aspects of my ex-partner that loomed large in my life. I believed that through prayer and fasting, things would improve; however, I gradually realized that my prayers were misdirected. Instead of seeking change in him, I should have prayed to make him receptive to change and for me to see my errors in longing to change what he had no desire to change.

During a journey with my closest friend and family, I was confronted with my partner's unpredictable conduct, which raised alarms about my well-being due to potential mental or physical abuse. Although my ex-partner never engaged in physical violence against me, his volatile outbursts were enough to instill a fear that hinted at the possibility of aggression. This fear echoed the disputes I remembered from my grandparent's home, where, despite the absence of physical fights, the tension was palpable. My parents' quarrels further reinforced my determination to avoid conflict in my own relationships. Whenever disagreements surfaced, I would retreat into silence, convincing myself that in the absence of physical harm, there was no abuse to acknowledge. This dismissal of mental abuse, which I reduced to mere name-calling or an assault on my autonomy, was a grave misunderstanding that would eventually take its toll on me. Not addressing this form of control and enforced silence led to a diminishing sense of self. I came to understand that my silence was not a sign of submission, but rather a delusion that I had lost my voice. In seeking guidance, I often turned to older, more experienced women, whose advice, though well-intentioned, largely reflected outdated notions of gender roles within a relationship.

Marrying at a young age and the desire to avoid becoming a mere statistic led me to make concessions in my relationship. The absence of children at that point in my life made me tolerate behaviors I would normally reject, all to evade the specter of loneliness. Yet, in truth, I was alone. While I supported friends and family through their parenting journeys, I faced the heartache of miscarriage in solitude, leaving a profound emptiness within me. Solo hospital visits during bouts of illness only underscored my isolation, casting shadows of doubt over my worthiness of love. The solitude that enveloped me following my father's death was deep, yet I navigated through it independently, maintaining an outward appearance of resilience. The loss of my grandfather carved a lasting emptiness that I found difficult to confront, choosing instead to remain quiet. This sense of fragmentation was not confined to my personal life; it spilled over into public spheres, where criticism chipped away at my self-esteem. Despite my efforts to conceal the hurt with a flurry of activities, academic pursuits, and professional commitments, true comfort came in the presence of my supportive network of family and friends. Their unwavering support and faith in my abilities served as a source of hope amidst the darkness of despair.

Our dynamic was marked by differing energy levels, with every conversation circling back to him and his egotistical disposition. His tendency to offer advice without applying it to himself further highlighted his self-absorption and hypocrisy. Being with someone who could not see beyond themselves made it difficult not to lose sight of my own identity. While the church emphasizes being equally yoked in faith, it overlooks compatibility in aspirations and mutual encouragement toward fulfilling one's full potential. When someone consistently disparages their partners dreams and beliefs, it's a clear sign of incompatibility. I have come to understand that someone's outward niceness can mask a lack of genuine emotional connection, which is detrimental to both parties.

As my health began to falter, manifesting symptoms that mirrored those of a heart attack, I was besieged by profound concerns over the future welfare of my children in my absence. My status as a single parent, or merely a single individual bearing another's surname, encapsulated my situation. In confiding with my God-sister about my relational uncertainties, I encountered her resignation to similar patterns in her own relationship, which only intensified my sense of isolation. Reflecting on 1 Thessalonians 5:23, it strikes me that while we often highlight the term "holy," we neglect the importance of being "whole." The pursuit of holiness seems incomplete without the foundation of wholeness.

Reflecting on the parable of the prodigal son in Luke 15:11-32, I found myself resonating with verse 17, where the son "came to his sense ."Like him, I realized I was in a place of spiritual destitution, engaging in destructive behavior to fill the internal void.

Reflecting on my proximity to completing a PhD in Trauma Counseling, I came to the profound realization that I, too, needed counseling. This led me to a path of introspection, seeking to unravel the origins of my behavior and the reasons behind the choices I had made. In what turned out to be our sole therapy session, it was evident that my partner's volatile temper was a formidable obstacle to the mending of our relationship. While I clung to the hope of mending our bond, my therapist cautioned me about the deteriorating situation and stressed the importance of personal development.

It was a bitter pill to swallow, recognizing that no matter how much one tries, the healing of a relationship is contingent upon the equal dedication and work of both individuals involved. However, my partner deflected responsibility, attributing the issues to me, thereby dismissing the necessity for change, and diminishing my mental health.

When I finally reached my breaking point, I decided to move out of our home while he was at work. I was careful and strategic as I moved in silence. Not one moment did I take into consideration my children's emotions; I had to think about myself and their future. With my newfound freedom, my health has improved, and I am now prioritizing self-love and personal growth. I walk with boldness and self-confidence.

Now, my transformation fuels my inspiration. I dream of founding a ministry named "Live Again," devoted to guiding individuals who have lost their way and reconnecting them with those who can teach them too truly live. I have launched my own venture as a mobile notary, also offering services to help others improve their businesses. I encourage my children never to let anyone curb their aspirations or hinder their pursuit of reaching their full potential.

Every breath is
a new arising,
a triumph over
trials.

Barbara Green

Barbara Green, a 69-year-old author, is a woman of many talents and passions. As she embarks on her third literary endeavor, she brings a wealth of life experience to her writing. Beyond her role as a mother and grandmother, Barbara finds inspiration in the pages of her Bible, drawing strength and wisdom from its timeless words. She is also a MaryKay Consultant, sharing beauty tips and empowering women to feel confident in their skin. Her warm smile and genuine care make her a trusted advisor to her clients. When she's not writing or consulting, Barbara can be found in her cozy kitchen, apron tied, and oven mitts at the ready. Her love for baking and cooking shines through in every dish she creates. From flaky biscuits to slow-cooked collard greens, Barbara's southern meals are a celebration of family, tradition, and flavor. Beyond her professional pursuits, Barbara is an active board member with ThriveHER Inc., a nonprofit organization dedicated to empowering women. She volunteers throughout the year, organizing workshops, mentoring young women, and fostering a sense of community. Barbara Green's life is a tapestry woven with faith, creativity, and compassion. Her words inspire, her actions uplift, and her spirit radiates warmth wherever she goes. Connect with her at bbsuga31520@att.net.

Healing in His Word: A Woman's Triumph Over Abuse

Barbara Green

The sun dipped below the horizon, glowing warmly over the quaint café where I first met him. His salt-and-pepper hair framed a face etched with wisdom, and his eyes held secrets—some whispered by time, others buried deep within. I was 25, and he was 42—a chasm of years that seemed insignificant against our shared laughter.

I believed in fairy tales back then—the kind where love transcends age, where gray-haired knights rescue damsels in their twenties. He was my knight, and I was his wide-eyed princess. His maturity promised stability, and I thought he'd cradle my dreams like fragile glass ornaments.

At 29, the heavens finally yielded. The job—the one I'd prayed for, applied for, and yearned for more than 11 years—unfolded like a rare blossom. Its petals held promises: financial security, a home for my two daughters, and the chance to savor life's sweetness. The job's wages allowed us to dream—to build castles in the air and anchor them with hope.

But life, that fickle artist, painted shadows across our canvas. The job, a beacon of light, also harbored storms. Its corridors echoed with masculine voices, outnumbering the women. My husband's jealousy, a tempest brewing, drowned reason. I pleaded, "I'm not betraying us; I'm weaving a safety net." But he clung to suspicion like a drowning sailor to driftwood.

Before my dream job, fate played its cruel hand. A seven-car collision left me battered; the car he'd supposedly gifted me crumpled like my hopes. And then came the beatings—the cruel calculation of rage. I hadn't handed him all the accident money; it wasn't much, but it was enough to ignite his fury.

We separated, and during those two months, I tasted freedom. But hope clung to my heart like a stubborn vine. I allowed him back into our home, believing love could mend the fractures. Yet the shadows deepened. His accusations—infidelity, betrayal—were shards of broken trust.

One moonless night, he left with a shotgun, intent on ending my life. Depression weighed me down, and I sought solace in solitary rides. I hid, breath held, praying for survival. In our bed, he asked if our marriage could work. I whispered a broken "no."

When he inquired if I wanted it to work, I found strength: "No." He didn't wait for explanations. Instead, he wielded a stick, and I glimpsed death's icy grip. My baby daughter, only 8, trembled in fear. Her innocence was shattered by the violence she witnessed. The next morning, my swollen face bore the marks of his fury.

I lay in bed, thanking God for sparing me, tears tracing the contours of my pain. My mother and aunt urged reconciliation, but I knew better. He'd beaten me twice, and I feared a third time would be my last. His twisted logic—jumping to defend kin—couldn't justify cruelty. I wasn't his mother or sister; I was someone's mama, someone's sister. I vowed never to endure such brutality again.

I divorced him, healing from the physical wounds. My career blossomed and I retired after 32 years, my resilience a testament to survival. Every day, I read Psalm 23: "The Lord is my shepherd." In the quiet moments, I found strength, and in my praise, I celebrated life—the one I fought to reclaim.

And so, I stand in the light, shadows fading. The Lord is my shepherd, He guided me through the valley of despair. Today, I am alive, a living testament to resilience. Through my season of growth, my daughters and granddaughters now know the strength that blooms inside of them is all and part of a staple to being a modern-day ThriveHER.

As I walked through my healing journey, I created opportunities to grow and be more aligned with God. Here, I will share some of the pivotal actions I took to get me to this point in life. Below read the details of when and how you should begin your healing journey after abuse, this is information that I wished I had known about when I endured the abuse and pain at the hands of my ex-husband.

I. Recognizing the Patterns

A. Acknowledge the Abuse

- Understand that what you experienced was abuse—physical, emotional, and psychological.

- Recognize the cycle of violence: tension building, explosion, and honeymoon phases.

B. Break the Silence

- Speak out: Share your story with a trusted friend, family member, or counselor.

- Seek professional help: Reach out to therapists, support groups, or helplines.

II. Reclaiming Your Power

A. Self-Care and Healing

- Physical recovery: Allow your body to heal from the beatings.

- Emotional healing: Process your trauma through therapy, journaling, or creative outlets.

- Spiritual grounding: Draw strength from your faith or personal beliefs.

B. Establish Boundaries

- Set limits: Clearly define what behavior is unacceptable.

- Learn to say no: Prioritize your well-being over others' demands.

III. Breaking Free

A. Legal Steps

- Restraining order: Obtain legal protection against your abuser.

- Document incidents: Keep records of any threats,

violence, or harassment.

B. Emotional Detox

- Cut ties: Sever all contact with your abuser.

- Build a support network: Surround yourself with people who uplift and empower you.

IV. Rebuilding Your Life

A. Financial Independence

- Job stability: Continue working and pursuing your career goals.

- Financial literacy: Learn about budgeting, saving, and investing.

B. Emotional Resilience

- Therapy: Work through trauma, self-esteem issues, and trust concerns.

- Self-love: Cultivate compassion for yourself; you deserve happiness.

V. Thriving Beyond Survival

A. *Empowerment*

- Education: Keep learning and growing.

- Advocacy: Share your story to raise awareness about domestic violence.

B. *Love and Trust*

- Healthy relationships: Seek partners who respect and cherish you.

- Trust your instincts: Listen to your inner voice; it knows your worth.

Remember, you are not defined by your past. You survived, and now it's time to thrive.

The Healing and Resilience

After divorcing my ex-husband, I redirected my energy towards healing from the physical and mental wounds encountered at his hands. As I began to heal, my career blossomed—into what would be 32 years of resilience.

Every day, I read Psalm 23: "The Lord is my shepherd." In quiet moments, I found strength and celebrated life—the one I fought to reclaim.

And so, I stood in the sunlight while the shadows of pain and brokenness began to fade in the background. The Lord is my shepherd, He guided me through valleys of despair. I was alive—a testament to survival. My daughters knew strength bloomed even in the darkest soil because I am a living testimony.

For years, I was ashamed to share my truth of abuse and survival. I often whispered my story inside but never outwardly. The dark shadows that once pierced my soul, and the sunlight that once fought to push through the storm are now behind me. God carried me through the storm so that I could share this story.

The Lord is indeed my shepherd, and I am so thankful for Him keeping me.

My journey is a medley, exquisitely pieced together by heavenly hands.

Alexandria Johnson

Alexandria Johnson is from the beautiful islands of The Bahamas. She enjoys helping people live optimally from the inside out. She has an Associate of Arts Degree in Psychology and Sociology, a Bachelor of Arts in Psychology, a Master of Science in Clinical Psychology, and a Master of Science in Child Forensic Studies: Psychology and Law. She is completing a PhD. in Christian Education. She completed specialized training in Mental Health and Psychosocial Support Co-Ordination and Substance Use Treatment for Adolescents and Adults. She completed certifications as a Cognitive Behavioral Life Coach, a Christian Life Coach, and Youth Leadership. For the past twelve years, she has used her training to help people across the lifespan who presented with mental health challenges.

She is an ordained Youth Pastor and Minister. She enjoys helping others grow spiritually and has received numerous awards for her ministry. For the past 15 years, she has been invited to speak at organizations both nationally and internationally. She has also been a featured speaker on webinars, podcasts, and talk shows promoting mental and spiritual wellness. She is a student of the elite Legendary Speaker Academy where she is mentored and coached by world-renowned speaker – Mr. Les Brown. She enjoys sharing messages of inspiration through writing. She is an International Best-Selling Visionary Author.

She enjoys serving others and instilling hope through her work. Connect with her at linktr.ee/aejohnson.

I Took Back My Power!

Alexandria Johnson

I was sentenced to death for a crime of yet unknown. From a very early age, I was locked up—in solitary confinement. I had no windows, bed, toilet, or small desk. I was surrounded by a wall of anger eight feet high. I took my place in a corner of the cell, sitting upright, with my legs toward my chest and my hands tightly around my legs. It was the safest place for me to be. There was a steel solid door that locked from the outside. There was only one key. My father had the key. He would open the door only to spew words of hate followed by ear ringing, and then shut the door. 'Monkeyface' was his favorite thing to call me, followed by an ear ringing that would trigger a headache. This continued for years. No one dared challenge him, or they would experience his wrath ten times worse. No one dared risk experiencing his wrath.

I realized early on that I had to fight on my own. I went to school and excelled. I went to Sunday School and was a model child. Yet, I was shackled and chained from my mind down. When my father wanted to have weekly escapades, he strung together the cruelest words and burned my mother down to ash. I knew what was coming next. We went running to my grandparent's house for safety for the weekend. By Sunday afternoon, he would be full of fun and wooed us back home. This paused when my father was charged and sentenced for a crime committed outside of the home. We lived with our grandparents. While living there, I realized that the light rays I saw forcing their way through the cracks were the love of my grandmother trying to reach me. I realized that the beams of love that challenged the eight feet were the love of Jesus.

As an adult, I realized a painful truth. It's almost as if it is a family curse. The women in my family three generations ahead of me never had a healthy relationship with their fathers. They lead lives being in relationships and marriages stained with abuse and infidelity, having more than one father for their children, or leading a lifestyle of drinking and using drugs. They struggled with their confidence and were too afraid to follow their dreams.

I was next. This curse wanted to write a scripted narrative for my life. The experiences that set this narrative in motion were happening. Abuse wanted to write my life story. The stage was set, and I knew the script. If abuse had its way, I, too, would have my turn. I would be in a relationship stained with abuse and infidelity, having children for different men, and or leading a lifestyle of drinking and using drugs. My abuse experiences sought to overwhelm me and force me to surrender to its power. These experiences sought to enslave me to its pain. I took back my power! I made God Commander-In-Chief of my life at seven years old. This was the best decision I made. By making this decision, I began anchoring my life. Though the winds and surges buffeted me, I weathered the storms.

I Took Back My Power From Negative Thoughts

Our experiences shape the way that we think about ourselves. My thoughts were shaped by my experiences with my father. Suicidal thoughts attempted to position themselves as the all-saving solution. Suicidal thoughts attempted to convince me that they were the only way out and that they could assist me in taking me away from it all forever. Self-depreciation thoughts were always on duty, reminding me I had little to no worth. Fearful thoughts reminded me that I was afraid and should be quiet. As I began reading God's word, I learned that God thought other things about me. I was in a thought war. I struggled to accept what God was saying about me because my mind was so filled with what my father said about me it seemed as if there was no room for anything else. I took back my power. Rather than squeezing it all in, I started deleting and emptying the trash in my mind. I surrendered my tormenting and whipping thoughts to the power of healing. I started deleting what my father said and replacing it with what my Abba Father said. This started a revolt. I was ready for my prison break.

I Took Back My Power From Negative Feelings

Our experiences bond our thoughts with feelings. I bonded with unhealthy thoughts shaped by my experiences with my father. I accepted these unhealthy thoughts as authentic and valid. These thoughts bonded with feelings of sadness, fear, guilt, insecurity, and shame. These feelings mixed in equal parts and became the total of my emotional experience and expression. I fought to exist while carrying these heavy and negative feelings. I stumbled and fell under the weight of these feelings, but I did not die from the crushing. I survived. I took back my power! I understood that God cared about my feelings and wanted me to be emotionally well. I accepted my power to manage my feelings. I consciously recognized that I could do something about my negative feelings. I went on an all-fruit spiritual diet and ate up the fruits of the spirit. You have that same power, too. You can do something about your negative feelings, too. Surrender your heavy and negative feelings to the power of healing.

I Took Back My Power From Negative Patterns Of Behavior

My thoughts and feelings influenced the way that I showed up for myself. Sometimes, I dared to be brave; other times, being brave was too hard. I needed to be perfect and reject parts of myself that did not represent ultimate perfection. Procrastination became the way I lived my life.

I was a loyal and obedient servant to my critical voice. I embraced self-doubt and accepted all that it said about me. I allowed people to exploit my talents and my kindness. I accepted the fears of others as my truth. Forgiveness tiptoed in and severed my bonds with negativity. I forgave my father, who caused me pain and forgave myself for the pain I inflicted on myself. I took my power from my father through forgiveness and recognized that I had the power to decide. I decided to fill my tank with gallons of self-love. I disputed irrational beliefs and dysfunctional reactions. Surrender your negative behaviors to the power of healing. Permit yourself to break free from negative behaviors.

Permit Yourself To Live Surrendered To Healing

God wants you to live a lifestyle of healing. I had to accept that for me to live a healed lifestyle, I could no longer have a conversation with my father until he was healed. My father would use a 'How are you doing?' conversation to finish serving you the venom he didn't get to serve you at the last discussion. He always has an extra serving of venom to share. God does not want us to be dominated by our experiences. He wants to heal us from the pain of our experiences. Jesus was pierced, crushed, and wounded to heal us. Healing is available for every part of us: pierced, crushed, and wounded. God wants us to thrive without limits and hindrances. He wants us to control our lives by deconstructing our old selves and accepting our identity crafted by Him. I fully surrendered to God's healing power and the professionals who helped me heal. I am now a conduit assisting others to activate the healing they need to thrive.

I took back my power through forgiveness and surrendered to healing. I felt safe and comfortable in relationships with my sisters, mom, aunts, female leaders, female mentors, and female friends. Following my healing, I felt relaxed and secure in relationships with males. I have been blessed to have healthy relationships with my brothers, uncles, male spiritual leaders, male mentors, and male friends.

I have been so blessed to have a partner who have been patient, gentle and kind and who kept his love constant and steady while I healed. I can remember the day, he said, "I am not your father; you are safe with me, and your father will not be able to hurt you anymore. I remember in that moment, almost instantly, the shackles of my pain began falling away and healing was stirred up. When we decide to take back our power, we activate a powerful healing process.

With every step, I claim triumph, for I am guided by illumination.

Dr. Cheryl Kehl

A world filled with stronger family units supports the much-needed ethics of generational prosperity, healing, and communal and global reconciliation. Leading the way by example is a compassionate advocate. Cheryl Kehl.

Cheryl Kehl is an Author, Cleric, Business Generalist, and a faith-based Family Coach, with a heart for broken women and domestic violence victims, facing substantial difficulties due to a history of diverse traumas. Moved deeply by her faith in God, Cheryl is a certified Christian Life, Intimacy, and Relationship Professional, in the business of seeing women reinstate healthy boundaries, enter into loving marriages, and sustain growing families; rooted in a relationship with Christ.

Cheryl's mantra is simple: she wants to reach women who have experienced hardships in life and bring them to an understanding that they can pick up and use what the devil meant for evil, to further the Kingdom of God. Cheryl is the host of "Walking in Greatness", a Talk Show on TakenTv, and also the podcast Walking in Greatness found on 19 different platforms.

Cheryl's love for domestic reconciliation is accommodated by regard for higher learning; as she has received both a Master of Arts in Business Administration and a Bachelor of Arts in Business Administration; with a concentration in Organizational Management. Cheryl is also a certified Property and Sales Expert, giving her the ability to properly convey to families, the importance of home ownership.

When Cheryl is not out volunteering and mentoring both women and families, she currently serves as a Chaplain to women at the Duval County Detention Center and looks forward to being certified as a Domestic Violence H.E.L.P. Coach, this spring. Inspired inherently by the people she meets every day, Cheryl is seen as a beloved member of her local community, a wife, mother, and cherished friend.

When she was 19, she got married and had a baby girl who was born one month premature. Cheryl and her husband lived in a 1 room studio apartment with their young baby. They were trying to learn at a young age how to be parents and adjust to this new life. Cheryl was used to growing up in a big home and attending private school, so this new life was so strange and hard for her. She went to the doctor for her six-week checkup and found out that she was yet pregnant again. She did not know how she would be able to survive financially with another baby within ten months with the lifestyle she had. At that time, she thought her only option was to have an abortion, which she did. This haunted her for years. She thought she was healed but found out in 2022 that she was not. She attended Forgiven and Set Free Abortion Recovery and finally, after 38 years, found the healing that was much needed. She volunteered at First Coast Women's Services for six months after that to help other women with finding hope and healing. Cheryl Kehl. Leader. Organizer. Advocate. Connect with Dr. Cheryl Kehl at cherylkehl@gmail.com

Bounced Backed And Healed

Dr. Cheryl Kehl

There were times in my life when I thought God was so far away and that He was not paying attention to what was happening in my life. There were so many challenging times that I faced as a child and into my adult life. The time that was scary to me is what I will share in this chapter.

In 1985, I was trying to escape a bad marriage and decided the way that I could make it happen for me and my children was to join the Navy. I gave custody of my children to a cousin while I went to boot camp. Once there I finished and was stationed in Jacksonville, Florida as my first duty station. I decided to end my marriage and start anew in Florida. During this time, I met a sailor and dated him for a few years. I got pregnant, and after many rocky relationship challenges, we decided

I needed to get out of the Navy and raise the three children while he remained on active duty.

In 1990, we were stationed In New Jersey at a Submarine base and living in base housing. This marriage became very hostile. My husband at the time was having an affair after an affair and had two other women pregnant at the same time I was carrying his child. So, I left him and went to a domestic violence shelter for four months and then moved back to New Jersey where my family was located. Once again, I had turned my back on God because He could not have possibly loved me with all these bad things going on in my life.

After leaving the shelter I received rental assistance for a year for myself and now three children. After the year was up, I found myself in a situation again where my children and I were going to be homeless, so I contacted the Navy and they put us in housing at the base my husband was stationed at. This was a really bad situation because I did not at this point have a job or a car. I had to do what I needed to do to provide a roof over my kids' heads. While the marriage was over, there was still a lot of fighting going on between the two of us.

I realized I needed to get aid to get out of my situation the day that I found myself and three children sheltered in a phone booth on the Naval Weapons Station in Colts Neck, New Jersey. Because of the ongoing marital abuse, I suffered a momentary nervous breakdown from the stress I was under. When I regained consciousness, I was examined in the emergency department. I knew life for me had to be different at that point. But it still took a while, and it was not until I was talking with the base counselor and told her I sat up at night thinking about how I could kill my husband and not go to jail that I was beginning to disconnect from my sanity. At that point, it went into motion quickly. Two hours later, I was in the back of a police car with my kids and all the things I could carry on my way to a battered-women's shelter.

I had family who said I could live with them and not go into the shelter, but they were four hours away, and I knew that would only be temporary, and I still needed help with counseling and getting my place to stay. During the time at the base, I was raped by my husband's so-called friend, who was supposed to watch out for us. When the investigation was going on for the rape, I had a cousin back home who was beaten and was on life support. I decided to go to my family and be there for them and was told the rape must not have occurred because I was not at the meeting with the military commanders and legal team during the investigation. So, it was shoved under the rug which happens so many times on military bases.

During my time at the shelter, I had my three kids with me and was pregnant with my fourth child. We got the emotional support and counseling we needed during those three months there. I met many women who had stories more severe than mine. This started my journey to want to help women escape abusive relationships and begin the journey of a new life. All I could think about was a scripture my mother used to say all the time as I was growing up - 1 Peter 5:7 "Casting all your cares upon Him; for He careth for you." As a child, I did not know what that scripture meant until I came to a point in my life where I needed to believe it. If I talked to Jesus about the things that were hurting me, would He do anything about it? I found out that once I believed it and gave Him the things that pained me without doubting that He could make things better - He did. Did all of my troubles go away? No, but life got better and better with each passing month.

After hearing so many stories in the domestic violence shelter, I could not believe some of the things I heard and was determined once I got on my feet I was going to help other women. I promised the devil that, the things he took me through I would somehow turn them into ministry opportunities.

Soon, I met a young lady in the church who asked me to go back to school with her and to get a counseling degree so that we could minister to women in the church who experienced domestic violence. I was just returning to church and getting my life together, I thought what a crazy idea. I did not see any women in the church who could need this help. She and her husband was in Ministry, so I said maybe someone confided in her and this was the reason why she wanted to help women who experienced domestic violence. So, years went by, and I never thought about it again. The young lady called me one day after I had moved to Florida from New Jersey to tell me she was being beaten by her husband. She said it had been going on for years and she hid it. I could not believe my ears. How could this have been going on and I did not know it?

It all started making sense, in our conversation years before about helping women in the church who were experiencing domestic violence. She was like me and wanted to use her pain and experience to help other women. We both wanted to let our pain fuel the ministries God had placed inside us. I soon lost contact again with her because she had to restart her life without her husband and life just got extremely busy and complicated for the both of us.

Growing up, my mother had a Goddaughter and I reconnected with her. Talking to her, she confided in me that she was going through domestic violence with her boyfriend, and she was afraid to have people help her because she did not want anyone to get hurt. About a year after our reconnection, she was stabbed over 100 times by her boyfriend, so she lost her life violently. This woke up a new determination in me to help women as best I could. I signed up to volunteer in a domestic violence shelter for about two years. This to me was not enough, so I knew one day I would start my work in the field of domestic violence.

As I thought about beginning the work, I started feeling ill-equipped, so my confidence level went down. Then I started researching the work and found that it looked like so many people were working in this field that I wasn't needed and started doing other things but still had this burning desire that I put on the back burner. I could not understand why I kept talking myself out of it. I started working with a life coach and she asked me many questions about things in my life I had suppressed. What I realized was that in my abusive marriage, I had addressed the physical abuse but never really addressed the things that he did and said to attack my self-esteem. The voices I was hearing in my head that I was not good enough or capable was not my voice but his. After that, I began reading scriptures such as Psalm 139:14 "I praise you because I am fearfully and wonderfully made; your works are wonderful, I know that full well." God created me as a beautiful and unique form of Him. I do not have to feel like I am less than anyone else.

One of the things that has helped me a lot when other people spoke negatively in my life is that I graduated high school at the age of 16. This happened because I am a very intelligent person. Once I found out I only needed to compete with myself, I understood I could do anything I put my mind to. God has placed a gift inside each of us and a work to do to glorify His kingdom, once we understand that we can be who He has called us to be. I want anyone reading my story to know and understand that you are special in the eyes of God. It is not clique that He does not create junk. He created each of us with talents and giftings that we need to develop and cultivate. My past does not dictate my future.

Another scripture that helped me understand that what I have been told – ' am good for nothing, no one wants me and that I will be poor, broke, and lonely the rest of my life is so untrue. I am being used for the kingdom of God and have been equipped to do the work according to 2

Timothy 3:17. God has equipped us to complete the work He has called us to do. There were some things that I had to do to prepare myself. You will have to do the same. Two years ago, I took a certification course, and I am now certified as a Domestic Violence H.E.L.P. Coach and have started a non-profit called R.I.S.E. Restoring Inner Peace & Self-Esteem in women who have come out of a domestic violence situation and ready to move forward in their life. I cannot even say this process has been easy and smooth. I have run into challenges with getting board members to stay committed. But I am equipped and ready to do the work that God has called me to do. I had set the work aside last year but being a part of this collaboration has reunited the flame inside of me.

There are times people think you cannot speak in their life because you have not gone through anything, so they think. God has a way of not making us look like what we have been through. For the next paragraph, I am going to be vulnerable and share some things that I have gone through that make me grateful to God for bringing me out.

At or around the age of 7, I was given away to my grandparents to raise. My father was married to another woman when I was conceived, so I was a hidden child. To this day at the age of 60, I do not know my father's side of the family. I did spend some weekends with his mother but was not taken around his family. Had many other struggles from a child to adulthood, because I didn't know what love looked like, I became a loose woman looking for love. Again, I was abused as a wife, raped, homeless for a few months, on welfare, had days when I didn't know how I was going to feed my kids their next meal. Days that I did not even have pampers for my babies and had to use towels. I tried drugs and alcohol to try and mask my pain, but it was not enough.

I thank God that I had enough sense at the age of 28 to come back to the Lord and surrender my life to Him. Guess what, I still had some hard days and still do but my outlook on it is so different now. I believe that things that I go through are sometimes things I cause on my own or things that I need to learn something from. I know that God has never left me alone. I have walked away from Him, but He has never walked away from me. If I truly look at my life, I have had way more good days than bad. Some of my bad days were low but those low times did not take me out. Even when I had a temporary nervous breakdown, God did not let it last too long. He allowed me to bounce back and live to tell the story. My story is so many other people's stories. Some just don't know how to get up and start living again. But my declaration to you is that God loves you and wants you to live and live more abundantly. He created you to win in this life, and if you live for Him, you will win in the afterlife. Stop letting your past hold you down. BE FREE!!!

I am a lighthouse of resistance, shimmering fiercely through the storms.

Joanne B. Lewis

Joanne B Lewis, MSSA.LSW is a native of Cleveland, Ohio. She is a servant leader with experience in higher education secondary school leadership. Joanne is a number one bestselling author, who has coauthored: Baldness with Boldness - Unmasking Alopecia and Revealing Resilience.

Joanne is a member of Alpha Kappa Alpha Sorority, Inc.

Joanne is a creative Christian woman seeking different perspectives bringing solutions to challenges of those she encounters. Joanne enjoys life with her husband, Albert Lewis, Jr. Ed.D. They have four children and eight grandchildren.

Joanne is affectionately called Gigi by their grandchildren. I dedicate this book to my angel Mommy Mrs. Armielee H. Ballard and Sister in love – Ernestine "Tina"

Ballard.

Contact Information:

Email: jblewis1908@yahoo.com

Website: iamjoanneblewis1.com

Facebook: Joanne B. Lewis

I.am.Enough.

Joanne B. Lewis

I detest the feeling of having no control over my life. For me, the feeling of no control equates to the old saying, "Got a foot on my neck." It evokes a sickening, oppressive feeling that I can see in my mind, my body tightens, and I start quietly breathing fast. Emotionally, I feel alone and moved into fight or flight mode.

There were many times in my life when I didn't have any control, as a teenager, no control over my emotions, felt sad all the time, didn't understand the mean comments from people who professed to love me, and had no control in protecting loved ones for abuse and cruelty, no control of simply not knowing where I fit in, and no control of how I would formulate my path in life to have a future.

When I told my parents that I wanted to go to college for Journalism, my father informed me that all I needed to do was learn to type and get a job. That was it, my mother had no say in the conversation. I was angry, he had never told me that he loved me, not one time. And when he did, it would be in my early fifties.

Psychologically, the impact of my environment mirrored what I would grow to learn was similar to other women in my life. They felt they had no way out, no love and support from others, so they suffered in silence and tried to make the best out of their situations. I vividly remember thinking one day, I wanted to be the person to help my mother and others in my family.

As I look back at pictures from my adolescent years, I have learned that I was a depressed teenager, I did not smile at all, but not today, I smile and laugh all the time.

I believe my saving grace came from the love of my beloved mother and my decision to accept Christ as my Lord and Savior at an early age. I have been told I have the soul of a person who has been in this life before.

I possess a spirit that intentionally processes any risk that would negatively affect me. This was a learned behavior. Growing up, I did not want to upset anyone at home, and I was never far from my younger siblings whom I fiercely loved then and now. I always stayed close to my mother, I felt like I was my mother's protector, she always told me that she loved me and that I was smart and beautiful.

I attended etiquette and modeling school. That came to a sudden stop for me, when a family member said to my father "Look, she thinks she's going to be better than everybody else." I tried to explain that I had not said or done anything. It did not matter, that was the end. Imagine the impact of that statement and how it affected my self-esteem.

Traveling through my life neither my sadness nor my propensity to not make waves would disappear. Do not get it twisted, my intentional risk aversion did not preclude me from eventually moving forward and putting myself and later my family first in every area of our lives. Throughout my teenage to young adult years, I would not make waves because of a deep-seated fear that something would be taken away from me that I valued, and I would have no control, this carried over through my career days.

I eventually married, had two children, and divorced. I always had office positions and yes, I learned to type very well. I enjoyed addressing customers' needs, and I along with my colleagues documented incoming calls and services. We were tasked with resolving concerns or complaints from customers. At the end of the day, we passed our worksheets to our supervisor. This process was repeated daily. There were times when customers wrote thank you cards for the service they received and expressed their appreciation.

During the employee evaluations, comments did not reflect anything positive, therefore employees would receive low evaluations. It was a never-ending circle, and I had no control over the process and did not feel I had a voice either.

I began to intentionally process my next steps. I was ready to get out of there. I had begun the process of taking control of my life. I initially wanted to become a teacher; my thoughts were that I could be home in the summers with my children. At that time, it was not feasible for me, the programs required the student to be a full-time student. I had two children, a mortgage, and a whole life. I looked at the field of psychology, and as I continued to process, I started thinking of what school I would attend that would "fit into my life."

I decided to schedule an appointment with a local university, and to my shock, the admission representative told me that I would be registered for remedial classes. Imagine my surprise, I asked her to explain exactly why she developed that thought as it pertained to me. Before she could speak, I had that "foot on the neck" feeling again. I informed her of my homeownership status and length of stable employment. She was unimpressed and barely looked at me. At that moment, I decided to leave and get her foot off of my neck. I was not going to be in any place where I was not celebrated. I was taking control of my life, no one was going to put me in a negative stereotyped box. I chose for myself and my family that we would not be a negative statistic.

I found a local adult degree college program, an evening program, which fit into my life. I went to the invitational meeting, which happened to be in the elementary school building where my mother attended school. I brought my young daughter with me. Even then it was important for me to show my children that their mother would create a new path for our family. This school accepted me because I was enough, and I valued myself as I began the process of my education.

This was not a painless process, I lived with sleep deprivation, PB& J sandwiches that I would eat on the way to class after work, and then after work while at my internship, and then to eat on the way home. I armed myself with the latest dictionary & thesaurus, and the current APA book, I wanted to understand what different words meant and gain an understanding of how they were used. I took so many notes, I eventually bought a small tape recorder, so I would not miss anything. There were no laptops, and no internet then, when it was time to gain more subject matters and draft papers, I would head to the library, find books, write notes, and check the books out to take them home for reference for my papers.

Throughout the years, I would go to work, no longer was I fearful, no longer did I feel less than, no longer did I need verbal acknowledgment from supervisors that I was doing an excellent job. I already knew that I had always served the customers well, and I continued to do so.

I faced challenges at home along the way by this time, my children and I were all in college at the same time. They were at different HBCU schools (Historically Black Colleges and Universities). Finances were always in peril, having enough money to transfer into the accounts, biweekly, sending clothing when they needed something, or money to go out to events at school, there were no cell phones, our long-distance phone bill was extremely expensive, and I wanted my children to call home whenever they wanted to call me. Fortunately, while I was at work, there was a toll-free number they would call me on if they needed me during the day.

I was determined that nothing was going to be too hard for me, I did not have to be fearful anymore. I accepted that I was empowered and in control of our destiny.

For the next four years, I attended both night and weekend classes, became a member of Psi Chi, the International Honor Society in Psychology, and had multiple Dean's list awards. Each morning, I would get to work, head to the cafeteria at 6:30 am, set up in the back of the cafeteria, and do my homework. Each morning, one of the cafeteria ladies would bring me orange juice and a biscuit. I tried to pay, and the ladies assured me that they saw me, and wanted to help me in any way they could. I am still appreciative of their love and support. At about 7:45 am, I would pack up my books and go into the office to start my day.

I learned that I was a good student, I delved into subject matters with energy in classes, it was a real struggle, being at work 5 days a week from 6:30 am to leaving work at 4:30 pm to drive to class by 5:30 pm - 8:30 pm and then drive home.

Nevertheless, I persevered, I kept a class chart of my classes from the first to the last class, with the start and end dates. Each semester, I would keep the previous course map and place the new one on top of the old one. I had a thick stack of reminders of my accomplishments. It was my reminder that I was an accomplished student, with academic merits including multiple Deans list certificates and being inducted into an honor society.

During the four years, I realized that not only did I have control of my life, but I also moved past the fear of someone taking something away from me. I knew that I was earning my education. I would tell myself and my children this mantra, two things could never be taken away from you, one is your relationship with Christ, and the second is your education. The more I thought and shared this with my children, the more I became fearless as I committed to my classes and studying.

I obtained a degree in secret from my supervisors. I also remembered the family member who caused me harm which led to my etiquette and modeling classes being taken away. No one was ever going to take anything else away from me. I was living by example, all while shouldering my responsibilities and attending school full-time, on my terms, my children would understand that, too.

To that point of living by example and teaching lifetime lessons to my children. My daughter is a special education teacher, she is starting her master's degree this summer. Her daughter is an HBCU graduate, her eldest son is an HBCU sophomore, and her youngest son is a ninth grader who has been inducted into the honor society. My son has earned his Doctorate in Education. His son has earned his Master's degree from an HBCU school and my son's daughter has earned her college degree from an HBCU. Both my children and grandchildren understood the education assignment. It is my prayer that my great-grandchildren will follow in our family tradition of first seeking God and then their education.

Each of my children has thanked me for the sacrifices that I made for our family. My children have recounted times of our shared experiences, and they said, "Mommy, we thought we were rich." I am grateful they did not see, hear, and understand my tears and feel my emotional and physical pain. They did not know the times I faced rejection when I needed help.

I am glad I serve a God who is faithful to His word. I knew that when utilities were disconnected and there was not enough food, that God would still provide for us.

I, along with my siblings and our children, cared for our mother until her 77th year of life. It was our mother who poured into us the love of

Christ, and how to live a life that would be pleasing to God.

God allowed me the opportunity to witness to my father the love of Christ, and I forgave him. I was in my fifties when I heard him for the first time, tell me he did love me and was proud of all my accomplishments. He showed me articles that he kept of me. He lived until he was 96 years of age.

I did it! I earned my Bachelor of Arts – in Psychology in four years with honors.

The next chapter was about to begin, and I was prepared, with no doubt about my abilities, no low self-esteem, no moving in fear of anything. I learned that I am valuable, I value myself, I have a voice and I use it. I first use my voice to give God glory for covering and keeping my family, I use my voice as an encourager and advocate for others.

I.am.Enough.

Dedication – I dedicate this writing to my beloved angels, "My Mommy" & my sweet Sister-in-Luv "My Tina."

My inwardness is an origin of hope, sustaining my path onward.

Dr. Sonya McKinzie

Dr. Sonya McKinzie is the CEO & Founder of ThriveHER Inc., a nonprofit organization established in 2016 to advocate for women affected by domestic violence and provide resources and tools to support them in taking their voices back. She is also a certified Trauma and Recovery Life Coach and has been honored with a Proclamation for ThriveHER Day in Brunswick, Georgia. Also, a multiple best-selling author who has written and contributed to over twenty books, she is a visionary author for the forthcoming Blueprint of a ThriveHER Anthology. Dr. Sonya is most passionate about her daughter who is also an author and her overall faith in God. Dr. Sonya loves empowering women and girls to create HUGE footprints that will make a mark on the lives of others positively! Connect with her at www.thriveher.me.

Shattering Shackles: Whispers In The Twilight

Dr. Sonya McKinzie

I was born and raised in Brunswick, Georgia, by a single, hard-working mother for most of my life. At the tender age of two years old, my father and mother divorced. From there, my mother and grandmother partnered to take care of me as my mother worked shift work at a local pulp and paper mill. My mother was a hard worker, a homeowner in her twenties, and a devoted daughter to my grandmother. My grandmother had several clients for whom she cleaned and cooked. When she was not at work, she was in church or taking care of me and my cousin. The events are vivid in my memory as if they happened yesterday. My grandmother was a devout usher on the usher's board at a Baptist church. We would be in church at least two times a week, attending church events with her. My grandmother did not go to college, but she was very smart, loving, and yet firm.

I grew up in a middle-class neighborhood that was filled with diverse families of all kinds, that looked out for each other, spoke, and engaged. Our neighborhood was peaceful, it was our home, and while small, it was filled with love and laughter. Between God and my mother, she made my sister and my life comfortable at the expense of sweat and tears. Thinking back to age eight or so, I recollect my mother marrying my stepfather. Sifting through the old, faded pictures from their wedding, I saw a little dark-skinned, sad girl standing beside her mother, watching as she exchanged vows with her soon-to-be husband and my stepfather. Gazing at my mother's face, she looked content but not thrilled. She exchanged vows with him in the end room of my grand-aunt's home, and that would be about the gist of what I remember from their wedding day.

Fast forward to the first time I heard my mother crying and screaming, saying, "I cannot breathe" I did not know what to do. I overheard my stepfather tell her, "I will blow your brains out". A part of me longed to pick up the phone and call the police or run next door to my Godparents home, but I was afraid, I was only eight years old. I did not know what he would do to me or better yet, what more he would do to my mother. Quietly, I lay sobbing and hoping that the door would open; I needed to save my mother from whatever that devil was doing to her.

The door opened, and I remember him storming out of the door and leaving. Once the back door closed, I slowly walked to their bedroom door and saw my mother lying there. She had her back turned towards the door, and she was crying. I climbed in behind her and cuddled her the way she did when I did not feel well or when I wanted to snuggle with her. I think I surprised her. When she turned over, I saw her face, and my stomach sank. Her face was not like the beautiful brown face I was used to seeing, it was swollen, and her eyes were bloodshot.

Thinking back to the time and space, I cannot begin to fathom how a child could have carried such a burden without breaking; I had to be strong to see my mom, the woman who was my hero and savior, beaten until she was black and blue. I do not recall the specifics, but I do remember that was not the only time I had to cover my mother with love and cuddles after being beaten by my stepfather. What I do recall is the day he left our home and moved into my grand-aunt's home, which provided him with shelter and a space to live while she attempted to reconnect my mom with her abuser, the devil.

It was not until I became a woman that I realized I had not healed from those memories of him beating my mother, sister, and me. We simply shuffled it away in our subconscious, I suppose. From that moment forward, my mother did not remarry, she dated but a marriage did not emerge from them. Instead, more heartbreak continued to dock her doorstep, and I, well, I continued to hope for a father figure who would treat me the way that little girl deserved to be treated. After years of broken dreams, I stopped looking for a father figure and started looking for someone to simply see me for who I was; a broken, dark-skinned, big-boned, and gap-toothed girl who was often the end of others jokes. No one saw beauty in me, after all, I did not see it myself. After my father called me ugly when I was a young girl, I was convinced I was ugly to the entire world. This is around the season when I realized the importance of a father's presence, in a young girl's life.

The Toxic Bond

When I turned sixteen, my mom gifted me my very first car—a Buick Celebrity. Its smooth white exterior contrasted with the rich burgundy interior. Little did I know that this car would become a catalyst for change, altering the dynamics of my high school experience. As the proud owner of a car, I suddenly found myself at the center of attention. Classmates who did not have vehicles gravitated toward me, eager for rides and newfound camaraderie. It was as if the Buick had granted me a newfound popularity—one that surpassed mere metal and rubber. But my newfound status came with unexpected consequences. A close friend introduced me to a shadowy enclave known as Dixville. Nestled within Brunswick, it was infamous for its illicit activities—drug deals, illegal transactions, and whispered secrets. Dixville was the forbidden fruit, tempting and dangerous.

One fateful evening after school, my friend requested a ride to Dixville. As I waited at the stop sign, the world outside my car window transformed. The air grew heavier, charged with anticipation. And then he appeared—a mysterious figure, lurking in the shadows. His eyes bore the weight of secrets, and his presence sent shivers down my spine. I hesitated, torn between curiosity and fear. What awaited us beyond that stop sign? Would this journey alter the course of my life forever? The Buick's engine hummed softly as if urging me to decide—to step into the unknown or retreat to the safety of familiarity.

In that fleeting moment, I glimpsed the duality of my existence—the mundane routine of school and homework, compared with the allure of danger and rebellion. The Buick, my faithful companion, held the key to both worlds. As I shifted gears, I wondered if this ride would be more than just a trip to Dixville—it might be the ride that defined my adolescence, steering me toward uncharted territories. Then the dark-skinned, hazel-eyed, silver-teeth-wearing guy leaned over into the passenger side of my car and spoke to my friend. Then he looked over at me and said "Hello, pretty blacky". Shyly I responded, "Hello". He continued to ask my friend if he could have a ride into Dixville and she deferred him to ask me since it was my car. After smiling at me with his silver grill, he asked, "Pretty Black, can I get a ride" and I responded "OK". That was the very moment I knew my life had changed.

Between the age of sixteen and twenty-one years old, Jacob and I became friends. It was ironic how different we were; he was a drug dealer with a nasty temper who could not seem to stay out of jail. And I, on the other hand, was a church girl who spent most of her time between school, church, and home. While he was incarcerated for several years, we corresponded by telephone and mail. I could not begin to understand what and why I connected with him. Perhaps, it was because he was the first guy to see me beyond my dark skin, awkwardly shy demeanor, and big bones, or maybe because my gap and crooked teeth did not seem to bother him, or it could have been the idea of a bad boy being interested in a plain Jane like me that made me fall for him. Either way, we spent years communicating by letters and occasional phone calls when the resources allowed. After about four years, he returned home from serving his time in prison. Much of me was afraid, and the remainder was excited to see this lifelong friend who had convinced me that I was loveable.

When I looked at him, all I could see was his brown eyes, silver teeth, and the cuts and scars on his face. However, while he appeared hard on the outside, he seemed to be gentle on the inside. Over time, our friendship continued to grow during the brief time he was out of prison. We later decided to try a relationship contrary to the odds that were against us. When that decision was made, I did not realize that it would be one of the worst decisions I would ever make. About a year or so into our relationship, the abuse began, and his verbal lashes transformed into physical hits and slaps. His jealousy revealed its ugly face, and instead of loving and caring for me, I became his punching bag. The man I thought would love and cherish me, became the green-eyed devil overnight. While in prison, he showered me with sweetest letters and words of encouragement, but when he was released, he was a different person. It seemed to be that I had chosen to be with a man who was internally identical to my stepfather. Thinking back, I remembered one night when he came home and was sweaty, and his eyes were filled with anger, or so I thought. Little did I know, he had spent the night snorting cocaine and marijuana with a friend of his. The money he claimed to have for me and our bills, was spent on drugs. I wondered how I did not know that he was addicted to drugs. How did I not know he was a womanizer? How did I not know he was a green-eyed devil? I also recall learning that I had contracted chlamydia, and it was from him. I knew it was from him because I had only been with two other men in my life, and that was years before him. When I discovered that he had given me a venereal disease, I was afraid and furious. I inquired who he had been with and advised that I had tested positive for a disease, he stated he had been faithful and that sometimes, the disease could be contracted through unclean semen, which was beyond me. It did not make sense, but I did not want to fight. I advised him to get treated and then left the conversation alone. Later that evening, I was driving to work and saw him past me with another woman in her car. Shocked by what I was seeing, I followed them and asked him, "Who is she?". He brushed me off and told me to go to work. Annoyed by the instance, I went to work and called my dear friend from work to discuss what had happened.

During our conversation, my ex-boyfriend came up to the job and banged on the glass door at the front of the building, begging me to open the door. Afraid of his actions, I became very anxious. My friend and co-worker continued to talk to and calm me down with her sense of humor and stories of her experience with abuse. She even offered to call the police, but I reluctantly declined.

The next morning after my shift at work ended, I decided I needed to know who this woman was, who he was in the car with, and whose baby was it that I saw in the car with them. Circling the area of Arco, a rough area of town in Brunswick, I looked for the car that I had seen the night before. Unsure of where I was going, I saw a man and asked for his help. It only took a few minutes before they figured out who I was talking about and pointed me in the direction of her home. Boldly, I walked up to the door of her home unsure of what was about to happen. I knocked on the door, and this short, red-haired, Caucasian woman opened the door and said "Yeah?". I responded and advised that I was looking for my then-boyfriend. She smirked and opened her front door, I looked over at the sofa, and around her home, I could smell a fragrance that was unfamiliar and yet, familiar. He was lying on a sofa, and the house was filthy, it reeked of marijuana. I began to call his name, and it seemed as if he was in a coma of sorts initially, and then suddenly, he woke up shocked by my presence. He looked at me and said, girl, get out of here. This is a trap, I sell dope out of this house. Not clear what that meant, I walked to the door, looked back, and then went home. At that moment, I was in disbelief that he had chosen drugs and another woman over our nearly decade of friendship and what I thought was love.

The Breaking Point

The phone rang around 3 p.m. CST or shortly after I had returned home from my second job. The woman that my ex had cheated on me with was calling me. It had been three days since the encounter, and I had not heard from him. So when I answered the call, I heard a voice on the other end of the telephone line, it was not the other woman, it was him. He said "Hey, baby, how are you doing?" as if the turn of events had not occurred days before. He explained that he was in jail, he and the other woman had gotten into a disagreement about me and ended up beating and sodomizing her. I could not believe what I was hearing, he had beaten and done some hostile things to her.

Then, amid the conversation, she began to share all of the

indiscretions that she had and laughed as if it were a joke. All I could think of was how sick and twisted their situation was; upon being released from jail, he came to my home, and we sat down and talked. He explained that he was

using the woman to sell drugs for him, and I responded with, when and why are you selling drugs, as he had been in and out of prison since he was 16 years old for selling drugs. After disclosing the information, I told him the only way we could consider working it out would be if he admitted himself into a drug addiction facility to help dry him out and get the therapy that he so badly needed. He agreed. I drove him to the facility, and it was not two days before the facility called me to come pick him up. He did not agree with the program and became so angry that he threw chairs and began fighting everyone who attempted to calm him down. When I arrived, he began to apologize profusely. He was covered in sweat and was annoyed; he was having some kind of reaction from not being able to use cocaine. I reminded him that, when we talked earlier, the requirement for us to even consider reconciliation was for him to complete a drug rehab.

Looking into his face, all I could see was a monster and someone that I thought I knew, but despite it all, I continued to speak and engage with him. Then one morning after I got off my overnight shift job, he came over to my house with one of his friends. He immediately began to demand that I fix him breakfast, and I promised him that I was tired. For whatever reason, my denial to cook him breakfast set him off, and he began to beat me in front of his friend. When he was done, he walked out of the door and left me lying there like a piece of discarded trash. I felt humiliated, embarrassed, broken, and manipulated. Again, I began to wonder how someone who loves me treats me the way he did. When people say that karma comes back on you, that is an understatement because within hours of that happening, he ended up going back to jail, but this time, he would be penalized and required to serve a minimum of 10 years of his life. Escaping the nightmare, I relocated to Marietta, Georgia, while he was in prison. With him being incarcerated again, but for an extended amount of time, I planned to relocate to Marietta GA, to escape his abuse and all things associated with him. The emotional scars lingered.

Reclaiming My Voice

After relocating to Marietta, courageously I began my path toward healing from the trauma and abuse experienced at the hands of my imprisoned ex-boyfriend. Writing and journaling became a refuge—a safe space where I could unravel the knots of pain, fear, and self-doubt that I carried deep within my spirit. Through self-reflection, I forced myself to confront the scars left by emotional and physical abuse. Each step taken was a step toward reclaiming my shattered self- worth.

In the quiet moments, I began to listen to my voice—the one that had been silenced for far too long. I further discovered resilience within myself, a strength that defied the darkness of my past. Rebuilding my self-worth became an act of defiance against the pain inflicted upon me.

Surrounded by supportive friends and mentors, seeking solace in their unwavering belief in my capacity to heal, I learned the importance of having a "tribe" that prayed for, encouraged, and comforted me.

My journey was not linear; triggers and doubts crept in on occasions, especially when I allowed someone to get close enough to embrace me. But I persisted. Reading books, journaling my thoughts, and practicing self-compassion for myself slowly rebuilt the broken parts inside of me.

The emotional wounds began to close, and I realized that healing wasn't about erasing the scars—it was about transforming them into badges of survival.

Today, I stand as a testament to resilience. My voice, once stifled, now echoes through advocacy work from Marcy's Law, my nonprofit organization, ThriveHER Inc., where I provide mentorship for other survivors of domestic violence and trauma. I now know that healing is not a destination but a continuous process—one that I navigated with grace, courage, and the unwavering belief that I am worthy of love and kindness and the name I now carry, ThriveHER.

Unexpected News

In October 2021, I received an unexpected call. When the phone rang, I heard a very familiar voice, however, the tone was somber and eerie. The person inquired how me and my daughter were doing and then began to tell me that my abuser had passed away while in prison. When I tell you, the emotions were complex—a mix of relief, closure, and a tinge of sorrow. There I was again, confronted with my past, reflecting on my journey from victim to ThriveHER.

I didn't celebrate his demise; instead, I focused on my healing, the forgiveness that I had communicated to him about ten years prior, and the empathy that I felt. It was at that moment and time that I realized how much I had grown. Instead of feeling relief, I felt melancholy about how his life ended and how much of his life he had spent behind bars. My prayer is that he found God and peace in his past before he took his last breath.

Grace, Growth and Gratitude

When I began to write this chapter, I did not have intentions of sharing this story; however, it was through connection, love, and support from the authors within this book that guided and held my hand towards sharing this part of my life. I am grateful to every one of them for helping me close this open chapter in my life. Through this project, I learned that my legacy is one of resilience, compassion, and empowerment. As the founder and trademark owner of ThriveHER Incorporated, I continue to guide survivors toward renewal, reminding them that they, too, can thrive beyond their pain. My daughter has had the opportunity to witness and participate in the fight against domestic abuse and trauma. I am proud that she gets to see my strength—a testament to breaking generational cycles and rewriting the narrative of survival. My story teaches us that forgiveness doesn't erase the past; it empowers us to shape our future. Through my passion for advocacy, I continue to speak against abuse and violence while fighting to ensure that survivors and victims do not walk alone on the path from victim to ThriveHER.

I am not just a Survivor; I am a radiant ThriveHER.

Lisa Pearce

Lisa grew up in Macon, GA. She was first married shortly after getting saved at a Christian school. We both fell out of church and were divorced two years later. Upon marrying my second husband, it became an abusive situation. She stayed married for 16 years and gave birth to three children. Her then husband had tried to kill them one night, but God delivered her and their three children out of the bondage. There were many hardships after that, but God saw them through, and blessings came after tragedy.

Today, Lisa knows her worth through what God's Word tells her. She is safe, healthy, loved, blessed, thriving, and growing. God aligned her path to cross with a wonderful Christian man, and they got married 14 years ago. Her husband reintroduced her to church and a restored relationship with God. She is currently writing a book about her life experiences. Her passion is sharing Jesus with others. Especially to the broken who don't feel loved. God set her free, and He is faithful in His Word which says the truth will set you free.

Lisa's hobbies include horseback riding, cooking, singing, reading, and listening to music. Connect with her at winston58@windstream.net.

From Bondage To Deliverance

Lisa Pearce

Slavery is an ugly word. It conjures up visions of humans shackled by chains. As a child growing up in middle Georgia, I knew all too well of the Old South's History. It was talked about in school and there were grim reminders around me. Not one, but two old Confederate statues were displayed next to a main downtown street. They had been there my entire life and were removed after numerous complaints were brought before the city and it was decided to relocate the statues to a cemetery that contained Confederate graves. And, I think of the old train station in Macon that still has the words "Colored Waiting Room" etched into the stone exterior. A chilling reminder of the unfair treatment and erroneous way of thinking that permeated the Deep South.

At the tender age of 8 years old, my family drove to a historic site about 40 miles south in the small town of Andersonville, Georgia. It was a hot summer day. There, right by the country highway, sat an old Union prison camp. The Union soldiers who were wounded and captured were kept there under deplorable conditions. Lack of medical care and lack of food were among some of the atrocities that these men faced. The museum had old black-and-white photos of the men. Their bodies resembled skeletons, emaciated and weak. I felt a sadness deep inside of me. As we exited our family car and walked down to a grassy meadow, I could feel a dreadful sadness around me in the place. It seemed that I could almost hear the anguished cries of men, smell the stench of the camp, and envision their lack of care, and the very obvious lack of humanity. I began to cry. It seemed all too much for me, the first realization that evil exists in the world. It was a memory that has been forever burned into my mind. At such a young age, it made a deep impression on me Later, as an adult, I visited Savannah, Georgia, the oldest city in the state. As an avid lover of history, I took many historical tours. I learned of the Irish immigrants who came across the ocean in ships during the potato famine. The Irish immigrants were indentured servants to the rich. I thought about my ancestors, who had passed down some Irish blood in my lineage, and who were simple sharecroppers, struggling to feed themselves. My granny would tell me stories about not going to school as a child, picking cotton all day long, and carrying nothing but a baked sweet potato in her apron pocket for lunch. Those were hard times, and it was before any type of government assistance existed.

I wondered what the difference was between a slave and an indentured servant. I learned that an indentured servant would work to repay a debt. They wouldn't earn a salary, but eventually, they would pay off the debt and be free from it. In contrast, a slave would be a slave forever.

There would be no hope of ever being free, and they would never be able to get out of their situation. A slave is often deprived of basic needs. A slave is shackled, maybe not physically by chains, but not able to be free. A slave is in bondage due to another person's influence on them.

I make this important distinction because as I approach the topic of domestic violence and abuse, we must understand how a toxic relationship can enslave us as well. It doesn't always happen overnight, but it's a slow process, and you are brainwashed as you keep moving out of the boundaries of the relationship. For instance, you may say to yourself, "Well, although he said something mean to me tonight, at least he didn't say or do this." And we draw a line in the sand on the behavior that we don't think is allowed. It may be that at least he didn't criticize my looks. Or at least he didn't get physical and hit me. But, then, the next time there is an argument, he does one of those things. And, you've just drawn a new line in the sand. And, the abuse continues to escalate. The control that the abuser has over you now increases. Maybe now you're no longer allowed to spend money so you can't carry a debit card. Maybe now you aren't allowed to work a job. Maybe now you can't wear make-up, or that dress that flatters and turns heads when you wear it. And, then, dear reader, you find yourself in a type of prison. You are constricted, stifled, and no longer thriving as a person. You see no way out of your situation. You are afraid of trying to get out. Your fear paralyzes you when you think about how you could leave. It all seems so hopeless, so impossible, and you realize that you truly are a slave in the relationship. But, here's the good news. Jesus is very clear in His Holy Word that the truth will set you free. He came that we may have life, and have it MORE abundantly.

I wasn't raised in church. I found myself sitting in a private Christian school as a 16-year-old teenage girl because my grades and behavior were both declining in public school. It turned out to be a blessing because I heard preaching from the Bible. However, it was a sort of legalistic type of church and school. There were lots of rules. I didn't understand all of that part. What I did understand was that I was born with a sinful nature and in need of a Savior who had already died on the cross and was risen again after three days in the tomb. He overcame death so that I could overcome my life struggles. I ran to Him. I went forward to a chapel service with a pounding heart. I felt an overwhelming relief as I welcomed Jesus into my heart. I knew then that my life had changed, and I finally had hope for a better life.

Fast forward approximately 18 years and imagine why I couldn't understand how I was now a prisoner in my marriage. I had gotten away from church after marrying my first husband. Ashamed to admit it, I had been unfaithful to him with another man. A man whom I thought was exciting, bold, and borderline dangerous. A stark contrast to the steady but mundane first husband. This new man had even coerced me into marrying him, and here I was, married to him now for 11 years, with three precious children, and the situation had slowly turned south. I was a stay-at-home mom and a homeschool mom. To make ends meet, I was constantly being told why and what we had to sacrifice. I couldn't have a car, so we shared one car. I couldn't have new furniture, or new clothes, or get a manicure, or go out to eat. It was all just too expensive. And, I didn't have access to the bank account. I was given cash twice a month, on payday, the first and the fifteenth. It was 2007, and for our family of five, I was given $225 twice a month to buy everything, including household items, and food. There was no room for error with cash. I carried a calculator and had to do without certain items. I learned to make food from scratch, including breads, biscuits, and cookies. I learned to shop sales, calculate the price per ounce, or pound, and spend every penny carefully.

We weren't allowed to have any pets, due to the expense. I recall how I went without a winter coat for years, being reminded by my husband, whom I began to think of as "The Bad Man", that if I bought a goodwill coat, it would take food out of my children's mouths. I had begun to resent these things about my life, and my children's lives. It seemed like everyone else had money to do things with, yet here we were, in a depressing and hopeless situation. I didn't have access to the money because he had the statements mailed to his job, where he worked in an office and could balance the checkbook and pay the bills while at work. I never questioned what he told me. If I did, I would feel guilty. I was constantly being reminded by him about how good I had it. How most women would just love to be able to be at home with their kids during the day. Whenever I would silently think in my head about him being "The Bad Man" I would feel guilty about that, too. When he snapped at me with mean words, it was because he was working so hard to provide for us. I just needed to be a little nicer and patient with him. When he came home, he told me about the stresses of selling insurance and earning extra commission for us, and how he had to work late to do that. I would thank him for what he was doing for us. If I had to tell him that one of the kids needed bigger shoes or a bigger coat, I would sense his anger, as he sat there silently, clenching his jaw, his pupils dilating as he drummed his fingers on the kitchen table, his thoughts somewhere far off, looking like a ticking bomb about to pop. I hated these moments, feeling like I was walking on eggshells, and silently praying that he wouldn't start ranting and punching things around the house. I had become skilled at hanging pictures over busted sheetrock, much like patching a band aid over a wound. Out of sight, out of mind. Hiding reality from any guests or visitors, however, few we had. And, hiding reality from myself and my children, not wanting them to see the holes in the walls any more than they had to.

The shoving, slapping, and punching would become more frequent. "The Bad Man" hit my mouth the morning that I was getting ready for the kids' dental cleanings. I looked at the blood in the mirror and saw my split lip. "Now, look at what you made me do. I guess you won't be needing the car this morning now, so I'll just drive myself to work." He wasn't even yelling; he was so calm and uncaring about my bloody mouth and my whimpering cry as I tried to stifle it because he didn't like it if I cried. I was too ashamed to go to the dentist that day, because I also had an appointment, and they would see my mouth. I was ashamed as I canceled all four appointments and the dental office expressed displeasure at not giving a 24-hour notice.

What a crappy life, I thought to myself. I wanted out, but, like a true prisoner, I could see no way out. No job would pay me enough to pay for childcare for three children. I wanted what was best for them, and "The Bad Man" had warned me about the abuse that would happen to the children if they were in daycare or public school. I was trapped. I prayed, even though I was out of church. I knew that Jesus was real, even though there were times that I had questioned it. I also stayed because I remembered in the back of my mind the preaching from church about divorce. It was wrong, it was a sin. I thought of one young couple where the husband had cheated on the wife. I thought that the Bible said that divorce was okay if there was unfaithfulness.

Yet, the church leaders had guilted that young lady into standing by her man, through better or worse, and upholding her wedding vows. If that was what church was about, then I wanted no part.

The night that Jesus busted open the chains of my marriage was a cold November night. Through a series of events, which included a gun being held to my head by none other than "The Bad Man", his threat to "blow everyone's brains out", and my failed attempts to leave with the kids due to being physically thrown over his shoulder and removed from the long hallway to their bedrooms, I heard a voice in my head, loud, forceful and stern, a voice that I didn't dare listen to, tell me "RUN." It wasn't fearful, it was said with authority and certainty. I couldn't leave the kids there, but I did. I ran out of the car and went to the police. And, that exposed the lie, the secret, and the abuse to the whole world. As awful as it was at the time, through this ordeal, I found my freedom. I found my children's freedom. We beat the statistics of domestic violence and I attribute it all to the goodness of God.

My worst fear was that others would know about my prison. My biggest deliverance was that others found out, protected me, and encouraged me not to go back. Jesus truly came to set the captive free! As I began to study my Bible and get back into church, it was revealed to me in Jeremiah 3:8 that God gave Israel a certificate of divorce for her unfaithfulness! And, God cannot sin! Jesus is clear in His word that if you seek, you will find. If you ask, it will be given to you. If you knock, the door will open. And, John 8:32 promises that you will know the truth, and it will make you free!

There is also freedom in forgiveness, and my three kids and I have been able to forgive "The Bad Man". We know that he has a sin problem, and we pray for him whenever we are reminded of him. I have now been blessed with a Godly husband who kept inviting us back to church until we went. He encouraged us to pray for "The Bad Man."

My dear reader, if you ever doubt if you can get out of a hopeless situation, please take heart and know that God is able to "do exceedingly abundantly above ALL that we ask or even THINK!" If we take that first step of faith, it will open up the universe for us!

One step sets off a chain reaction of events that God will orchestrate on our behalf. He works ALL things for good for those who love God and keep His commandments.

I wasn't in church when my miracle happened, and I wasn't living right, but I know that I prayed to God for help, and he came to rescue me right in the middle of the mess. He will do the same for you!

My soul is shatterproof, forged in the fires of my trials.

April R. Randall

April R. Randall is an attorney with over 15 years of experience. She is a government relations professional and etiquette enthusiast. April is committed to community service. Her parents instilled the importance of helping others at a young age.

April has always had a passion for writing. She has had several poems published as well as legal articles. April has always wanted to write a memoir, but fear held her back. In 2023, a dear friend of hers passed away. This friend always told her "Renée, tell your story." After learning about the untimely passing of former model and Forest Whitaker's wife, Keisha Nash from anorexia nervosa, April knew it was time to tell her story – not for herself, but so that she can help other women, particularly African American women.

A graduate of Wellesley College and the University of Baltimore School of Law, April resides in Montgomery County, MD with her husband, David, and son, Ryan. Connect with her at april.renee@gmail.com.

My Friend, Anna

April R. Randall

"Take a look at yourself and then make a change." Michael Jackson," Man in the Mirror. Growing up, I used to love Michael Jackson and "Man in the Mirror" was one of my favorite songs. As a young girl, I used to sing this song all the time. Like Michael, I struggled with the image looking back at me in the mirror. I was repulsed by my reflection. When I looked in the mirror, I saw an overweight girl who was too disgusting to bear.

I was obsessed with how I looked. To be fair, I did not always feel this way. Before my teen years, I was a "happy go lucky girl". I was an only child and I wanted for nothing. My family was not wealthy, but my parents ensured I had everything that I needed and wanted. I was truly the "apple of their eye".

My parents always made me feel beautiful. Even though I was a chubby girl, they told me I was pretty and smart. I believed them because who did not believe their parents? I worked hard in school and my grades reflected that. School is where I excelled.

Although my parents told me I was pretty, I never really believed it. Who were they kidding? I was the fat girl with pigtails. However, it did not bother me as a young girl very much. As I long, I made my parents proud by getting good grades, I did not need anything else. I knew I could become anything I wanted to be when I grew up, so long as I worked hard and got good grades. I always wanted to be a lawyer. That was my goal and kept my sights focused on it.

I wish becoming an attorney was always my primary goal. Sadly, that was not the case. By the time I was a pre-teen, being smart and getting good grades was no longer good enough. I wanted to be pretty too.

Growing up, I was chubby. Let's face it, I was fat. A childhood friend used to make fun of my legs because they were large at the top and slim at the bottom. He used to refer to them as "turkey legs". I hated that. My male cousins called me "Baby April", which was sweet when I was younger. By the time I started high school, "Baby April" was no longer acceptable. The nickname reminded me of a plump baby. Teenage boys were not interested in dating a baby. They wanted the good-looking girls like they saw on TV.

I loved watching beauty pageants on television growing up. I never missed a pageant. Ms. America, Ms. USA, and Ms. Universe were queens to me, and I wanted to be like them. They were so pretty and everyone likes beauty queens. I used to see advertisements for pageants for girls and teens. I wanted to apply so badly so that I could eventually become Ms. America, Ms. USA, or even Ms. Universe. I wanted to apply and compete in Florida, which is where these pageants usually occurred. I did not even consider the cost associated with pageantry. I wanted to do it. Yet, this would not come to be. It was not the money or the competition itself that prevented me from applying, it was me.

Did all the pageant contestants and winners look alike? No, but they were all skinny. Unlike today, there were very few African American women competing in beauty pageants. Yet, that did not bother me. What bothered me, and prevented me from applying, was that I was not skinny like them. Regardless of their race, education, or background, they were all skinny. This helped to crystallize in my mind that being thin equalled beauty. I was not thin, and thus, I was not beautiful. Since I was not beautiful, I clearly could not apply to compete in a beauty pageant. So, I did not.

Do not get me wrong, people used to tell me I was cute. "Cute" is a word used to describe puppies and babies. You are cute as a toddler or in elementary school. You may even be cute in middle school. However, it is not cool to be "cute" in high school. In high school, the most popular girls were pretty; not cute. The popular boys did not date "cute" girls. They dated the pretty girls, not the cute ones. Even my friends would tell me I was cute. Yet, being "cute" was not good enough for me. Yet, there I was. April Randall, "the cute girl".

As I got older, when someone called me cute, they would invariably focus on an innocuous physical feature, such as my eyes or smile. Other times, they would focus on something I was wearing, such as a cute sweater or handbag. They never complimented me for myself, or if they did, it was a left-handed remark, such as "Oh you're cute for a big girl." That was me — April " cute for a big girl" Randall.

I truly hated being referred to as "cute for a big girl". Although I would laugh and smile when people said this to me, I would cringe on the inside. As they say, laughing makes a difficult easier pill to swallow. So, outwardly I would laugh while crying inside.

When I think about my closest girlfriends growing up, it makes me smile. They saw me at my highest and lowest. I recall my mother telling me, "April, everyone is not your friend. You will be able to count on one hand the number of friends that you have." This was true when I was growing up. I had friends from elementary school Cy Cy and Jay and my middle and high school friend, Sam I loved these girls. We were thick as thieves until we were not. When I met the new girl, Anna, the summer before my junior year of high school, my relationship with my old friends changed.

Anna was amazing. She was everything I was not – skinny, pretty, and popular. So, you can imagine my surprise when we met in high school, she was interested in being friends with me. I was skeptical at first. A girl like her did not ordinarily want to be friends with someone like me. At best, they would talk with me just enough to copy my homework. Yet, that was not the case with Anna. She excelled in school. Like me, Anna was an honor roll student. Unlike me, however, she was thin. Anna was PERFECT. Therefore, it did not make any sense for Anna to want to be friends with me.

I never learned why Anna wanted to be friends with me, but I am glad she did. Although I remained cautious for a long time; waiting for her to move on to the skinny popular girls. Thankfully, this never happened and Anna and I became best friends.

As best friends, Anna and I did everything together. We studied together, shopped together, and went to the movies together. We even liked the same books. She liked William Shakespeare and reading about Greek mythology like I did. Ironically, Wuthering Heights was her favorite book, too. We were the ideal friend pair.

Shopping together was tough, however, because she was able to shop in the junior section of department stores. Anna was even able to purchase clothes from the boutique, 5-7-9, which catered to the smaller girls. Not plus-size girls like me. We were relegated to the plus-size section of J.C. Penney.

I used to talk to Anna often about how much I disliked how I looked because I was overweight. I cried with her about it countless times. One day when I was talking to Anna about how hated how I looked, Anna said she could help me. It was kind of her to care about me; certainly no one else had.

I accepted Anna's offer to help me and did she ever! She was like my trainer and dietician all in one. We exercised and dined together. She motivated me in ways no one ever had. Initially, Anna encouraged me to stop eating certain foods, particularly carbohydrates, all meats, and dairy. Then I switched to diet sodas, water, and black coffee. While dieting, Anna helped me with my exercise routine – two or more hours of step aerobics a day. We eventually progressed to eating only two meals a day and then down to one or none at all. Of course, I was exercising feverishly the entire time.

Anna said that if I followed her strict diet and exercise routine, I would lose weight. Of course, she was right. The pounds melted off quickly. I started to lose weight and friends and family took notice. When I returned to school for my junior, the kids would stop me and tell me how nice I looked. The guys started to hang out with me more, including some athletes. Girls were asking how I lost weight and if could I help them.

It was funny how I went from being the fat, ugly girl that people ignored, to the one they all wanted to know. This would not have been possible without Anna. Thank you, Anna.

Soon, I was hanging out exclusively with Anna. I still liked my other friends, but Anna was my new best friend. She understood me the way they did not. If it were not for Anna, I would not have lost weight and my peers would not have accepted me. Oddly, if my parents thought this was an unhealthy relationship, they never said anything about it.

The fat girl who used to wear a size 16 was now wearing a four and shopping in the same stores as Anna, such as 5-7-9, or in the junior's department of J.C. Penny's. Good riddance plus size department! To this day, I still remember how exhilarating it felt when I was able to confidently walk into 5-7-9 and purchase a pair of jeans. I did not have to hold my stomach in to zip up the pants. I did not break into a sweat when I pulled them up. I had succeeded!

Although I had lost weight like I set out to do. I went from about 150 lbs. to 100 lbs. in three to four months. This, however, was not good enough. Anna, who was my friend, became my competition. I idolized her, but I wanted to be better than her. I wanted to win!

If Anna suggested we exercise for an hour a day, I would do two. If she said let's have six crackers and a Diet Coke, I would have four. If she said "Let's only eat two meals a day," I would eat one or none. Who needed food, anyway? I needed to beat Anna!

My weight began to drop rapidly, and my schoolmates and family noticed. Before, they were complimenting me, but now they were talking about me. They thought I was sick or was using drugs, which was absurd. The D.A.R.E. (Drug Abuse Resistance Education) program from elementary school scared the dickens out of me. I had no desire to use drugs.

I did not care what they had to say. Teenagers are always talking negatively about each other. My family did not know what they were talking about. I looked good! Who cares that my bones poked out and that if you touched me you might feel a bone? They were all just jealous. They did not have the discipline that I had when it came to diet and exercise. Even the "skinny popular" girls could not go into the store, 5-7-9, and purchase clothes in the size 00. I felt that I was special because my size was not even the name of the store. The girl who was non-existent to others when I was fat was wearing a size that would suggest that I did not exist. The irony!

During this time, I did not care about much else aside from losing weight and getting into a good college. I continued to excel in school, and I was excelling at losing weight. Everything was great; so, I thought. Yet, I had begun having panic attacks. I could not sleep. Oftentimes, I would wake up panicked in the middle of the night. I also became anxious during this time. I was afraid of eating with people because I did not want them to judge me for eating. I was also cold all the time. Even if it was 70 degrees in the house, I wore at least two layers of clothing. At some point, my mother realized I had not had a menstrual period. I could not recall the last time I had my period. It did not bother me at all since I did not want a baby. Yet, my hormones were all out of sorts.

By the middle of my junior year, I started to notice fine hairs all over my body, including on my face. No matter how often I plucked them, they came back. I also started to experience dizzy spells and feelings of light-headedness. I was lightheaded from not eating, but before I could eat, I needed to count the calories. I was a pro at this. I knew the calorie count of everything that went into my mouth. Anna taught me that of course. She taught me everything she knew.

Anna helped me because that is what best friends do. She taught me how to relieve the pain and what caused the pain in the first place. Anna told me that I had to do the latter first; so, I did. To help me, she introduced me to her cousin, Beulah. Beulah was okay, but she stayed to herself. She and I did not become as good of friends as Anna and I were, but we were associates. Beulah told me how I could rid my body of the food I had eaten with only a toothbrush. If I ate something, I was able to force myself to regurgitate by sticking the toothbrush down my throat. I did not like this very much though because I loved my beautiful teeth. Instead of making myself regurgitate, I began taking the laxatives that she suggested. The goal was the same – to get rid of the food as quickly as possible. Bye-bye, unwanted calories.

During this time, anxiety and panic attacks were not the only things I was experiencing during this time. I was sad all the time. I experienced bouts of loneliness and the feelings of unworthiness came back. It did not make sense because I felt unworthy when I was fat. I was skinny now; so, this should not be. I would get upset with myself when I gave into hunger pangs and ate something. I did not know what to do. Anna to the rescue.

Anna showed me how I could relieve the emotional pain I was experiencing. Rather than using a toothbrush, I required a blade. I still remember the first time I ran the blade against my skin. The trickle of blood flowed out like the tears I cried every night. The funny thing is, the pain only went away for a short time. What resulted was my doing it again and again and again. The razor might have left scars, but who cared? Nobody saw me. They never did. Nobody cared about me – the fat, ugly girl.

I was wrong. Somebody did see me, and they cared. My family saw me. My family cared. After New Year's Day when I was 16 years old, my mom and Aunt Gloria took me to meet visit a doctor whose office was at a hospital. My mom said I was just going for a checkup. Liar! This was not a checkup. I left my home that morning and did not return until a month and a half later. After checking my pulse and noting that my heart was beating at less than 50 beats per minute, the doctor told me I was at risk of a heart attack and that I needed to be admitted immediately because tomorrow was not promised to me.

I was terrified. All I could think about was missing school. I had work to do and tests to take. I was a straight-A student. I could not miss school. I had to keep my grades up so that I could go to college. Plus, I was scheduled to take the SAT in a few weeks. This was not in the plans.

What about my friends, especially Anna? Could she visit me? I could not do this without her. She was my best friend. Anna had been with me for months. We were always together; thick as thieves. Of course, she could at least visit me in the hospital.

Although I could have visitors, the doctors would not allow Anna to visit me. Why? I asked them. Why could my best friend not visit me in the hospital? I did not even know how I could endure staying in hospital with people I did not know, without being able to see Anna. Please, I begged. The doctors refused. They refused to allow Anna to visit me or for me to call her. I was at a complete loss. It was all so overwhelming.

Anna had been my support blanket, and now I could not see or talk to her. I was upset with the doctors. I was upset with my parents. How could they do this to me? It was not fair!

After a day or two of being in the hospital, my social worker, Lucy, sat me down and said Anna was not my friend. She said Anna had lied to me. Lied to me? About what, I asked. This woman did not even know Anna.

Lucy asked me if Anna had ever told me her real name. I looked at her like she was crazy. I said, yes. Her name is Anna. She told me that was not true. She said Anna's name was Anorexia Nervosa, and that she had been known to kill people. Kill people? This social worker was nuts! She went on to ask me if Anna had introduced me to her cousin, Lemmy. I told her she had. Lucy said Lemmy's real name was Bulimia Nervosa, and that she too had been known to kill people.

I could not believe it. I refused to believe it. Why would Anna, my best friend lie to me and try to kill me? That did not sound like her. I could not believe Anna wanted to kill me. We were friends.

Yet, after days, weeks, and over a month in the hospital and not seeing Anna, talking to my therapist, and attending group sessions, I came to realize that Lucy was right. Anna/ Anorexia Nervosa was trying to hurt me. She preyed on my vulnerability and pretended to be my friend. It was a farce. I came to realize that she did not care about me at all.

Even though I knew Anna treated me badly, she was still my friend. I did not have many friends left because when I was sick, I isolated myself from friends and family. When I thought I was all alone, I still had Cy Cy, Jay, and Sam. They were there for me when I was discharged from the hospital despite having distanced myself from them for months. Yet, Anna was there for me too. She apologized and said she was only trying to help. I forgave her, but the deadly cycle of excessive dieting and exercising started again.

It was not until someone found me nearly unconscious in my car in the parking lot of the supermarket that I finally realized that I needed help. Here I was parked, in front of the place that sold the items that I thought would kill me – food. I was not healed, and because I was not healed, I was not free. Something needed to change! I wanted to change. I had so much to look forward to, including going to my #1 choice for college.

I decided at that moment I would commit to recovery. I was scared, but I knew I could not live this way any longer. I knew it would be difficult and that I would regress during my recovery journey. Yet, just like I committed to losing weight, I would commit to getting to a "healthy weight".

It was and still is not easy. I struggled for a long time. By the grace of God and the support of my family and friends, I am here. I could not have done it without them. I regressed often. If I am honest, I am still struggling today. Yet, I have the tools and strength to fight back. Most importantly, I have my son. After nearly 10 years of not menstruating, meaning I could not conceive, he is here - my miracle child. If for no other reason, I am determined not to go back to that dark place for my son.

Anna continues to come around now and then. The negative thoughts that haunted me as a teenager plague me to this day. Strangely, I am grateful for Anna. It seems odd, but as they say, what does not kill you makes you stronger. I went through hell because of Anna, but along the way, I found strength and determination to survive. With the support of my parents and family who prayed for me, my friends who were there for me, and my therapist, I was able to make it out of the horrific period.

Today, Michael Jackson's lyrics hold a new meaning for me. "I am starting with the [wo]man in the mirror. I am asking [her] to change [her] ways." The change I am making is to love myself for who I am; no matter what, because I am worth it.

I release the bonds of past harm, encompassing the light of healing.

Maresa Roach

Maresa Roach, with her radiant smile and vibrant personality, is a beacon of positivity. Despite a past marred by hardship and disappointment, she transformed her life through faith and determination. As a teenager, she struggled with self-esteem issues and dropped out of high school. However, at 42, she returned to education, earning her high school diploma and later a Bachelor's of Social Work from the University of District Columbia.

In 2022, Maresa became a best-selling co-author in the book anthology "Faith for Fiery Trials: Volume III," where she shares her journey from trauma to triumph. Her faith, she says, carried her through the fire unscathed.

Maresa's strength lies in her ability to empathize with those in pain and her commitment to her community. She has a special place in her heart for victims of domestic violence, sexual assault, mental health issues, substance use disorders, and homelessness. Her past experiences have made her a beacon of hope for those in need.

Maresa's part-time role as a Customer Service representative was where she first recognized her calling. Strangers would confide in her, often returning to thank her for being a ray of light in their darkest times. These testimonies of how God used her past pain to help others still move her deeply.

Maresa, born in Lorain, Ohio, works as a Youth Engagement Specialist and Resident Service Coordinator in the District of Columbia, addressing mental health, substance abuse, and social deterrents. She is a living testament to the power of transformation - turning shame into shine.

Her community service and career as a change agent are extensive, including work with Sasha Bruce Youthwork, Christian Tabernacle Church of God, House of Ruth, and more. She has served seniors, volunteered for So Others May Eat (SOME), and even earned a service-learning trip to Cape Town, South Africa, while pursuing a Master of Social Work at Howard University. Maresa truly embodies the spirit of service and transformation. Connect with her at:

FB-@maresaroach
IG-@maresaroach
X-@maresa_roach
Website-www.maresaroach.com

Thriving From The Heart Of Hurt!

Maresa Roach

My Storms turned into Rainbows…Destined to Survive and Thrive through pain!

Thinking back on my life, I realized that I have always been destined for greatness. The torture, pain, and disappointment that I endured was all a part of the result. God saw fit to turn my trauma into triumph. A part of me believed that I was destined to fail. I hadn't seen the light at the end of the tunnel for so many years until I committed my life to Jesus Christ!

I was on a journey of self-destruction for many years. I recall attending Howard University School of Social Work and how overwhelmed I was with schoolwork, finances, living situations, and low self-esteem. All of these things resulted in my being diagnosed with major depression and generalized anxiety. During my tenure at Howard University School of Social Work, I was having difficulty committing to the workload, and retention of information was not the best, so I requested that my IQ be tested.

Although I was working towards earning a Master of Social Work, I wasn't fulfilled. Unknown to me, I had not dealt with and healed from the trauma that I endured as a 15-year-old girl.

When I was a little girl, I suffered from so many insecurities, and truth be told, those insecurities seeped into adulthood. My father was murdered while I was in my mother's womb. Longing for the father I never had I wanted to be loved by a male figure. I was looking for love and in all of the wrong places. At the tender age of 15 years old, I lost my virginity. You see, I liked the neighborhood boy who lived on the corner from where we lived near the corner store. He was cute, so I thought, and I wasn't allowed to talk to many people, let alone boys. So, when I was allowed to go to the corner store. I'd make it my business to cross the street where his house was. I was a naïve kid, so as he gave me the attention, I thought, we began to talk. One evening I noticed him, and he asked me to come into his house. This was an evening before my mom, sister and myself were going to church. I ended up going into this guy's house and the rest was history. We had sex and quite frankly I didn't enjoy it. It was then that I realized I missed what I never had, a male figure in my life. I wanted someone to love me for me. I began a pattern of dating men that didn't care for me, but for what they'd get from me. I didn't have a father, and in turn, my relationships with men were a trickle-down effect of me looking for love in all the wrong places, as I mentioned in the book, anthology Faith for Fiery Trials, Volume III. I am a survivor of sexual assault. Sexual assault at its worst. It is one thing to be raped, but to be raped by several boys and men is another story. The traumatic experience left me alone, afraid, skeptical, and not trustworthy of people. Not just men but people. I have always been friendly and, at times, a bit naive.

After the rape, I became a promiscuous girl. Here lies another scenario of trusting a guy who didn't have my best interest at heart. I was ashamed and felt it was my fault. I was fifteen years old. I liked this boy and went to his house to hang out. I didn't know where things would lead. I just wanted him to like me. When I got to his house. We began to kiss, and one thing led to another. He suddenly got off of me, and out of nowhere came several boys and one older guy forcing themselves on me. It has been so long ago that I did not remember how many there were. I just knew there were more than three. After the incident, I was in a state of shock. I did not remember how I got home. It is all a blank. I was violated, but after the incident, I refused to tell a soul. The pain was deeply rooted in my body. An indescribable pain. Years went on and I would often see one of the boys. The older boy was mean and cruel to me. He would holler out "You're a freak booty" when he saw me in the streets. He taunted me for years with mean words. He eventually stopped the torture. He was murdered. I must admit that when I got the news, he was dead, a part of me was happy. He tormented me for so many years that I was glad I no longer had to suffer.

Although he was dead, the stench of the sexual assault lay dormant in my mind and heart. I dated guys and slept with them not because I enjoyed it but because I felt a sense of self-gratification to please them. It seemed as if the relationships I sought after were a cycle of pain, hurt, and suffering. I didn't share this information with anyone until I was 42 years old. For years I was ashamed and thought it was my fault. Eventually, I forgave myself and the men that violated me. I gave it to God.

In these next few sections, I'll speak about three situations that occurred in relationships that were key to my life. I will share how adult men took advantage of a little girl, turned hurt woman who believed she had to please men to be happy. I remember meeting a man one day while I was skipping my 10th-grade class. An older guy who had no business dating a 15 maybe at the time 16-year-old. He had to be in his mid to late 20s. He was a semi-professional boxer, drove a car, and had his own apartment. I was flattered to be hanging out with a man who had it all together. So, I thought. How would I know any better? I wasn't experienced or mature enough to understand. Later, I was told he preyed on young girls and eventually, I stopped seeing him.

A year later, I met this older man who lived in my building. He was at least 55–60 years old, big, burly, and extremely tall. I don't know how he introduced himself to me or how it started, but what I do know is that this man saw the fearful, naïve little girl who wanted no part of obeying her mother's stringent rules. He knew I wanted to get away from my mother. He knew the challenges my mom and I were having, and he used the vulnerable little girl's family issues to prey on. He used drugs, alcohol, money, and gifts to woo me as if he had my best interest at heart. Later, he'd ask for favors. I wasn't interested in him. But at the time I thought it was a safe space and a place to get away from my mother's strict unrealistic, self-loathing ways to keep me bound in the house. We didn't have outings, no time with other kids, and I was bored and unfulfilled. My life just seemed so unfair. I sought love in all the wrong places. This man used me and pretended to care for me. I felt alone and lacked love and attention from my mother. We had sex, and I hated it. I regretted it but chose to indulge him. Eventually, I was forced to have sex with him again, and when I didn't want to, I was beaten, and sexually assaulted. Because I didn't have anywhere to go when I didn't meet my curfew at home. I begrudgingly knocked on his door. There were times I slept in the hallways of the apartment building where we resided, when I couldn't get in the house. I was running from home because I was unhappy. I ran from unhappiness to pure torture! I felt alone in every sense. I had no one to turn to. By the grace of God, I fled from the toxic relationship. Never looked back. He died many years ago, and I hadn't had any thoughts of the trauma until my sister mentioned it a couple of years ago. I mentioned it to my therapist, and she responded. "You never shared this with me" I wasn't ready to do the work and held onto the shame.

Some years went past before I dated anyone seriously. I was just living by a prayer and a wing. I felt lost and all alone, so I became promiscuous. I slept with men not because I wanted to but because I wanted to make them happy. I became addicted to drugs and alcohol for some time…feeling like no one loved me. I was living a life of sin, homelessness, and downright, downtrodden. I was delivered from drugs and alcohol. But I didn't fully give my life to Jesus Christ. I got a job and met a man whom I thought would be my husband. I was in my mid-twenties, twenty- four to be exact. I dated this guy for about 5 years. He was tall and handsome. He seemed to be a pretty decent guy. There were some red flags, but when you are attracted to someone, and looking for love in all the wrong places… you ignore the signs. There were subtle signs that warranted he wasn't on the up and up, but not screaming abuse signs! Eventually, he began to show signs of abuse.

He was controlling, to say the least. He'd watch (tree boxing) me through a window while I was at work, follow me to work, monitor the type of clothes I wore and how much weight I'd gained or lost. If I changed my diet or he thought I was trying to lose weight, he'd question me. He was an insecure, scared, man who thought every man that looked at me wanted me. I allowed it because what I didn't realize was trauma had me in a chokehold, so much so that I feared being alone. I didn't know how to live without living through the need to have a man in my life. I was bound with insecurity, and the need to be loved. He was a Christian man, a deacon in the church and supposedly saved, and filled with the Holy Ghost.

The straw that broke the camel's back was when he attempted to hit me after a Wednesday night church service or choir rehearsal in the church. I had some popcorn in my hand, and he knocked it out of my hand. I knew we were heading in the wrong direction in this relationship. He once hit me in my ear as hard as he could. This incident happened in front of his mother. I feared him and what he might do to me. It was then I knew I could no longer tolerate the physical, emotional, and mental abuse. One Sunday after church, I told him I could no longer see him. He walked me to my apartment and said, "You can't leave me, I'll kill you"

I later found it was a generational cycle. The men in the family were abusive emotionally or physically due to their home life, as they witnessed their mom be a victim of abuse. This man was the youngest of 17 siblings and witnessed the abuse, so he became an abuser. There was a controlling spirit like no other within him, and he took all of the pinned-up frustration out on me. I pray for those who are thrivers and survived the torment of being abused. I pray for the accused and ask God to cleanse their hearts. I pray for the accuser that has been the victim and uses their hurt-to-hurt others. The accuser needs just as much love as the victim. I realize there is no sense in hating those that have hurt you. The saying goes, hurt people, hurt people.

I CHOOSE TO HAVE A HEART FILLED WITH LOVE AND FORGIVENESS.

In 2020, I decided to live a life of holiness and abstain from sexual immorality. I've had a problem with abstaining from sex in the past due to the strongholds and trauma I've endured. But I have committed my life to Jesus Christ, and he has made it all possible. I trust in the Lord with all my heart, pray, fast, read the Bible, and have weekly visits with my therapist. These are the tools I have in my toolbelt to kill the wiles of the enemy when he tries to distract, tempt, or slither his way into my heart and mind. I won't turn back and can't turn back!

God rescued me for such a time as this! I share my story to provide some hope for the hopeless. I was bound by a life of sin, shame, hurt, pain, addiction, promiscuity, and abuse! I survived it all. It took 41 years of my life… to solely surrender my heart, mind, spirit, and soul to Jesus Christ.

God can do the unspeakable when you trust in HIM. I didn't have confidence due to past hurt. I was ashamed and didn't believe I'd ever get my life back on track. In 2022 I became an Amazon Best Selling author of a book anthology, Faith for Fiery Trials: Volume III. I share my story with woman that have survived/ living in domestic violence relationships and facilitate groups. I am a motivational speaker, and a podcaster. I've been featured in magazine articles, social media live broadcast, and interviews. I'm sold out for Jesus Christ, and I want you to know that no matter the challenges in your life. Give it to the MASTER. He will give you peace in the midst of the storm, HE will give you joy in the midst of sorrow. For many years I'd envisioned myself speaking to a multitude of people, and had no clue when, where or how this vision would transpire. But what I do know is God made it possible in HIS time.

I am a THRIVEHER!

Scriptures from the Heart

Psalms 73:21 (ESV)

My flesh and my heart may fail, but God is the strength of my heart and my portion forever.

Philippians 4:7 (NIV)

And the peace of God, which transcends all understanding, will guard your hearts and your minds in Christ Jesus.

Psalms 37:4 (ESV)

Take delight in the Lord, and he will give you the desires of your heart.

Matthew 6:21 (NKJV)

For where your treasure is, there your heart will also be.

Proverbs 4:23 (NIV)

Above all else, guard your heart, for everything you do flows from it.

Resources

National Council for Mental Well-Being

http://www.thenationalcouncil.org/

Better Help

http://www.betterhelp.com

Psychology Today

https://www.psychologytoday.com

Suicide Prevention

If you or someone you know is in crisis, contact the Suicide Prevention Lifeline at

1-800-273-TALK (8255), or dial 911 in case of emergency **Sexual Assault/Rape**

Rape, Abuse & Incest National Network (RAINN)

https://www.rainn.orgNational Sexual Assault Hotline

1-800-656-4673

Domestic Violence

https://domesticviolence.org/

I am complete, not for the absence of scars, but for the story they reveal.

Ra'Nesha Taylor

Ra'Nesha Taylor is a beacon of transformation and empowerment, illuminating pathways to self-realization and personal metamorphosis. As a devoted Transformational and Spiritual Life Coach, Author, and Creative Entrepreneur, she guides women on soulful journeys of self-discovery and holistic growth. Ra'Nesha's work is a testament to her deep commitment to empowering women to step into their power and embrace their brilliance unapologetically. With a holistic wellness and business management background, she brings a unique blend of expertise to her coaching practice, fostering transformative growth on every level - mind, body, and spirit. Through her deep introspection and healing journey, Ra'Nesha discovered her true identity and purpose, inspiring others to do the same. Her mission is clear: to ignite the flames of empowerment within women, guiding them fearlessly toward lives of authenticity, fulfillment, and joy. Connect with her at www.helloranesha.com.

A Journey Of Healing And Self-Reclamation

RaNesha Taylor

As I sit here at my great-grandmother's dining table, the soft sounds of jazz playing in the background, I find myself in a trance of gratitude. Reminiscing on just how far I've come, I can scarcely believe the winding path that has led me to this moment of peace and purpose.

There was a time not long ago when my life was plagued by a constant sense of turbulence - an endless cycle of mental, emotional, and physical anguish that left me feeling utterly lost and depleted. The more I tried to ignore the limiting beliefs and deep-seated insecurities that held me back, the tighter their grasp became, until I found myself drowning in a sea of unworthiness, inadequacy, and self-loathing.

The darkness I encountered during those years was truly all-consuming. Monthlong bouts of functional depression would leave me in a state of emotional shutdown, unable to even bear the sight of my reflection. I would sit in the darkness, lights turned off, mirrors blocked, my voice silenced, saved for the mandatory interactions of the workday. An entire hurricane raged within me, yet my outward demeanor remained stoic and emotionless - a mask that only served to further the feeling of being unseen and unheard.

I battled these limiting beliefs and emotions for the majority of my life, allowing opportunities to pass me by and never fully pursuing my aspirations or desired improvements. At least once a month, I would have a moment of profound self-questioning, wondering what was wrong with me and why I was in such constant physical, emotional, and mental turmoil. Since I was 11 years old, there hadn't been a single day where I wasn't in some form of pain. Something was always hurting, and it was exhausting.

I remember the days of my childhood when I used to spend countless hours daydreaming and fantasizing about my future life. I had all of these grandiose dreams, aspirations, and visions of exploration and wanderlust. Mapping out plans to touch every corner of this earth and learn about as many cultures as I can. Being young, I had so many desires that I could never stick to just one. I used to fantasize about more than just my surroundings. I also imagined what my life would be like without the constant pain and sadness. What does it feel like not to feel trapped inside my body? What would it feel like to be free?

It was as if I had imprisoned myself within the confines of my mind, shackled by a lifetime of trauma and negative experiences that had whittled away at my sense of self-worth. I knew I had to break free, but the mere thought of facing those deep-seated wounds felt utterly paralyzing. How could I begin to unravel the tangled web of mental and emotional blockages when the mere act of looking in the mirror filled me with such profound disappointment?

I had a feeling that something was off, but I couldn't quite put my finger on what it was. I felt lost and overwhelmed, and I knew that I needed a change. I knew I had a problem, but I was too exhausted from surviving to figure out a solution. I constantly gave my all to everything and everyone around me, but I never took the time to give myself the love, attention, and care that I deserved.

The mind-body connection was inextricable, and the physical toll of my internal turmoil became increasingly apparent. Chronic pain, debilitating gastrointestinal issues, and hormonal imbalances plagued my days, a constant reminder of the profound impact that suppressed emotions and limiting beliefs can have on the physical form. I found myself in a constant state of dis-ease, my body reflecting the discord that reigned within.

I didn't know how to begin to address my issues because it meant facing and possibly reliving the trauma that I experienced, some being self-inflicted, meaning that I had to take full responsibility for my life regardless of how I got to the state of misery I was in.

As each year of my twenties slipped by, I grew increasingly restless, yearning for the change that had eluded me for so long. I would question everything - what was going on within me? Why was I in so much pain? During this time, I was working jobs that drained me emotionally and physically, often finding myself in tears before entering to clock in. I knew the path I was on wasn't the one I wanted, but I felt lost, unsure of which direction to turn.

What I did know was that I couldn't continue to bury my pain and leave it festering, spreading roots so deep that it infiltrated every dimension of my being. I knew if I didn't do something, I'd spend more years existing in misery instead of living in fulfillment. I often asked myself, especially around my birthday, 'Do I want to spend another five years living like this?' My answer was always an emphatic 'NO!' followed by a quite expressive tangent with the most colorful language. At this point in my life, I had to make a decision. To either continue life as it is or take the steps toward change.

So, I am almost 27 years old and it feels like I am constantly being sent through this loop of spinning around the drain. At one point,

I couldn't find a way out, but I knew that I refused to give up. I refused to allow the mental blocks, trauma, pain, and disdain in my life to take me down.

As 2020 drew to a close, my life reached a critical turning point. Trapped in a soul-sucking job that only exacerbated my mental and physical decline, I found myself at the edge of a precipice, teetering on the brink of a complete unraveling. It was then that a profound realization struck me: I could no longer continue down this path of self-destruction. I had to take back the reins of my life, no matter how daunting the task may seem.

It was during one of these bouts of self-reflection that I realized the true root of my suffering: the refusal to confront the darkness and burdens that had taken up residence within. And so, with a mix of trepidation and determination, I embarked on a tumultuous yet transformative journey of healing and self-reclamation. I knew that to break free from the shackles of my past, I would have to face the deepest, darkest corners of my psyche - a prospect that terrified me to my core. But I also knew that, if I wanted a chance at true fulfillment and freedom, I had no other choice.

Over the next few years, I descended into the abyss, peeling back layer after layer of the trauma, limiting beliefs, and negative self-talk that had held me hostage for so long. I explored the depths and crevices of my mind and my emotions – my entire being.

Everything that I had buried, locked in my internal vault had come to the surface. But I knew this was necessary to get to the taproot of the blockages.

It was a dance with sanity, as I wavered between moments of profound clarity and utter despair, serenity, and serendipity, or calamity and confusion. There were times when I wanted nothing more than to give in to the overwhelming urge to let the darkness consume me once and for all.

But something deep within me refused to let go – to surrender. I knew that if I kept persisting, if I continued to surrender and trust the process, eventually I would emerge from the shadows, reborn and empowered. And so, I kept going, even as the trials of fire threatened to break me. I had to go it alone, isolated for nearly two years as I navigated the uncharted terrain of my psyche.

Through it all, I clung to the belief that there was a deeper purpose to my suffering - that my journey of healing and self-discovery was not just for my benefit, but for the sake of others who might be walking a similar path. I felt a calling, a conviction that by sharing my story, I could offer a beacon of hope and inspiration to women who might be grappling with their versions of the darkness I had faced.

And so, as I peeled back the layers and shed the burdens that had weighed me down, I found myself stepping into a newfound sense of purpose. The more I embraced the truths of my own experience, the more my awareness and consciousness expanded. The love I held for myself, for my life, and for the divine source that had brought me to this moment, grew exponentially.

It was not an easy journey by any means, but with each triumph over the forces that had once sought to defeat me, I felt a profound shift. The limiting beliefs that had kept me trapped in a cycle of self-loathing began to crumble, and in their place, I cultivated a deep well of self-trust, self-confidence, and unwavering self-belief.

Where once I had been consumed by feelings of unworthiness and inadequacy, I now radiated a sense of purpose and belonging. The pain and struggle that had once defined my existence had been alchemized into the very fuel that propelled me forward, fueling a deep desire to not only heal myself but to empower others in the process.

As I embarked on this transformative journey, I began to recognize the profound interconnectedness of the mind, body, and spirit. I realized that the mental and emotional blockages I had grappled with for so long were not only manifesting in my physical well-being but also permeating every aspect of my life. By addressing the root causes of my suffering, I found that I was not only cultivating a newfound sense of self-love and acceptance but also unlocking doors to greater personal and professional fulfillment.

One of the most significant realizations during this time was that, my experiences were not just for my growth, but for the benefit of others as well. I felt a deep calling to share my story, to be a beacon of hope and inspiration for women who might be navigating their versions of the darkness I had faced. It was this conviction that ultimately drove me to carve out a space for myself in the wellness industry, where I could authentically share my journey and empower others to embark on their paths of self-discovery and empowerment.

Today, as I reflect on the journey that has brought me to this point, I am filled with a profound sense of gratitude. It is through embracing the darkness that I have truly come to appreciate the light, and it is through sharing my story that I hope to illuminate the path for others who may be walking in the shadows.

My work is not just a career, but a calling - a passion project born out of the ashes of my transformation. It is a testament to the power of self-reclamation, a beacon of hope for those who have felt trapped in the confines of their minds and bodies.

Like the phoenix rising from the flames, I have emerged from the depths of my suffering, stronger and more resilient than ever before. It is my greatest hope that, by sharing my story, I can inspire other women to embark on their journeys of healing and empowerment, to shed the shackles of the past, and to step into the fullness of their divine potential.

My heart of hearts
is a continual oceanic
machine of self-love, from
which I draw bravery.

Made in the USA
Columbia, SC
21 August 2024